DEFILED ON THE
AYEYARWADDY

One Woman's Mid-life Travel Adventures
on Myanmar's Great River

by Ma Thanegi

Defiled on the Ayeyarwaddy
One Woman's Mid-life Travel Adventures on Myanmar's Great River
By Ma Thanegi

Copyright ©2011 ThingsAsian Press

Photographs by Ma Thanegi
Editing assistance provided by Janet Brown
Cover and book design by Janet McKelpin

Please be advised that restaurants, shops, businesses, and other establishments in this book have been written about over a period of time. The editor and publisher have made every effort to ensure the accuracy of the information included in this book at the time of publication, but prices and conditions may have changed, and the editor, publisher, and author cannot assume and hereby disclaim liability for loss, damage, or inconvenience caused by errors, omissions, or changes in regard to information included in this book.

For information regarding permissions, write to:
ThingsAsian Press
3230 Scott Street
San Francisco, California 94123 USA
www.thingsasianpress.com
Printed in Singapore

ISBN-13: 978-1-934159-24-8
ISBN-10: 1-934159-24-7

Contents

This book is for my brother
Captain Edwin Aye Tut,
a Master Mariner who once rode the ocean waves.
Among the alumni of our Methodist English High
School, many know me only as Edwin's Kid Sister, and
I bear this name with pride.

Preface

I have always loved the Ayeyarwaddy River and am not being overly mushy when I confess this. Many writers and poets of my country have declared their passion for this river in mountains of poetry, good and bad, and there are unending references throughout our literature. The Ayeyarwaddy is known as Our Mother River, and since Myanmar people are religiously devoted to their mothers, a river given this name is truly up there, on par with the top-level, high-echelon celestial beings.

I was once astonished to read an English-language coffee-table book about Myanmar, in which a writer airily began her short article by saying, "Since the Burmese never write about the Irrawaddy, it is up to others to do so." Well, madam, I thought in amusement, if just the bad poems written about our river were all put together, their weight could squash you to death, regardless of your size.

Legends say that in the beginning of time, the Great Creator Spirit took a cup of gold in his right hand, a cup of silver in his left. He scooped water from the Great Ocean many miles away and poured it onto the high northern mountains. The water from the gold cup became the male Mai Kha River, with the female Mali Kha River flowing out of the silver cup.

Mai Kha and Mali Kha have different personalities. Mai Kha is shallow, bright in the sunlight, rushing with happy chuckles, fast, aggressive, and loud, but Mali Kha is deep, silent, dark, slow, and mysterious ... and dangerous. Near the confluence where she meets Mai Kha to form the Ayeyarwaddy, she flows slowly, but her strong currents and rapids can drag a body down in a minute. High cliffs and boulders the color of dried blood cast dark, foreboding shadows upon her as she passes.

Strangely enough, I love her willful mood changes and deep silence more than I love her brother's happy chatter. But then maybe it is not so strange, because purgatory for me is traveling with companions who chatter without cease.

In his book titled *Return to the Irrawaddy*, Frank Kingdon-Ward, a botanist who collected orchids and rare plants in this region in the mid-twentieth century, said the area between the two rivers has a range of mountains running from north to south, but with more on the eastern, or Mai Kha's side. Up to seventy miles from the confluence, the peaks rise to no more than 9,000 feet, but beyond that the range "erupts into a group of peaks nearly 12,000 feet high."

During his collecting forays in the area, he had often glimpsed one river or the other, roiling in white foam down a gorge, at times dropping through "an unending series of violent rapids."

Like an icy crown on the very tip of Myanmar is the highest ice-capped mountain in Southeast Asia, 19,316-foot Hkakaborazi at the eastern end of the Himalayas. She is a mountain of black rock covered in blue-white ice and has been conquered only once, in 1996. After April, the melting snow of this Himalayan peak swells the waters of the Mali Kha and Mai Kha rivers. From their union, the Ayeyarwaddy is born.

This new river then heads west to find herself barred from further travel by a high hill named the In Khaing Bon, which keeps the Ayeyarwaddy from flowing straight westward into India and prevents Myanmar from being a desert. Meeting the hill head-on, the river makes an almost ninety-degree turn and goes north, then takes a meandering detour to flow southward again. She runs for thirteen hundred miles and at the delta branches into seven rivulets which flow into the sea.

After I wrote *The Native Tourist: In Search of Turtle Eggs*, I longed to ride the Ayeyarwaddy right from its confluence in the Kachin State to where its waters flow into the Indian Ocean. By the time I was able to begin this expedition, I was a different person from that earlier author, older and wiser than the woman who, giddy with optimism, had traveled through Myanmar by bus to make a pilgrimage.

It was impossible for me to ride the river in one trip, so I made the journey over several years and on various vessels.

Now that I have accomplished this goal, I earnestly hope I never get the urge to climb our ice-capped mountains in the north at the tail end of the Himalayas.

An Introduction to My City and Me

I have lived in Yangon all my life but I always feel as if I am just visiting. Mandalay, I often think, is my true home. It is the city of my ancestral roots and my mother's birthplace, across the Ayeyarwaddy from where my father was born, and not far from Shwebo, where I was.

For us Burmese there is forever a strong pull to the place "where one's afterbirth was buried"—never mind that I left mine behind at the age of eight months. But even as I write these words, I know I am seriously deluded: the heat and dust of a Mandalay summer would kill me in two weeks.

Besides, the Mandalay people I know, or am related to, have the most exquisite and gentle manners, while my lifelong stay in Yangon has made me brusque of manner and impatient in speech. Every time I am in the presence of Mandalay-bred people I feel like a bull just about to step into a china shop.

Yangon, for all the denial I have of belonging here, has had a strong hold on me in all aspects of my life, for my whole life. It is the place where I have gone through what I call my various entities: willful child, sullen teen, frantic painter, dignified wife of a Myanmar diplomat, party-animal divorcée, political prisoner, and writer. What a life ... or lives ... I've had in this place. I wouldn't change a thing.

Yet my happy delusion of not being at home in Yangon makes me feel as if I am still discovering this city, especially when I keep losing my way on streets that are far from my usual routes. For me, discovering a place anywhere in the world means checking out cultural sites and food, sometimes not in that order ... and it's due to the depth of my interest (or rather, of my stomach) that I keep discovering great food in unexplored corners of Yangon through the goodness of people who keep opening new restaurants.

My three college friends Nu Nu, Wendy, Dahlia, and I go on Food Discovery Forays every two months or so all over Yangon, looking for that certain place we have heard about that offers great steamed crab or excellent Shan noodles or succulent roast duck or spicy chicken with paratas, the fluffy Indian pancakes. After a leisurely lunch we tour new upscale department stores, grinding our teeth in fury at the displays of youthful, trendy fashions because we never saw such things under the Socialist economy when we were young enough to wear them. My friends and I buy sedate clothes or fabric or groceries; they buy trinkets for their grandchildren, and I for my maid's four daughters. I drive my aging Toyota along routes that are new to me while the others keep up a running navigational directory: "Go straight here! Now take the next left! Stop! It's a red light!"

I live in a small flat in a run-down, garbage-strewn housing estate near Chinatown where the sidewalks on both sides of the street are thick with vendors. There is a morning bazaar along a dirt lane just half a minute's walk from my place that draws me daily with its cheap monhinga noodles and soft mont pyit thalet pancakes. It must reveal something about my concept of home that I hanker for monhinga, the fish broth and rice noodles of Yangon, almost every day and only eat mondhi, the thick rice noodles with chicken that is a Mandalay dish, about once a week. The mont pyit thalet pancakes—savory rice batter cooked on open pans with a sprinkling of coriander, boiled peas, and sesame seeds—are also originally from Mandalay, and are for me a twice-weekly fix.

A block away along the sidewalk there is an evening market where I can find everything—chicken vermicelli soup Mandalay-style, fruit, flowers, fresh meat, fowl, noodles, cheap clothing, costume jewelry, slippers, salt fish, potatoes, bags of charcoal, and grilled chicken.

When I'm exhausted from a day spent running errands, this is where I go for my favorite comfort food—chicken salad. It is made from an entire boiled chicken, bright yellow with turmeric. White and brown meat, entrails, liver, gizzard, skin, heart, feet, neck, head, and wings are all chopped up—including the bones. It's mixed with a handful of raw cabbage strips, sliced onions, chopped green chillies, and julienned citrus leaves; seasoned with salt, tamarind paste, and a squeeze of lime; and finally is augmented with a scoop of thick chickpea soup. This makes a hearty dinner for one thousand kyat, the equivalent of one U.S. dollar.

My trips to downtown Yangon lead me to uneven sidewalks lined on both sides with plastic sheets spread out on the ground that serve as shops. In the evenings there is hardly room for two pedestrians to pass each other—the first passerby has to balance on one foot, trying not to topple into a pile of jeans while the other squeezes past, careful not to trample the nearby bananas.

The shops I like best are the ones with piles of different stuff, "Anything for Five Hundred." When I was a child the selections of toys that they offered were treasure troves where I would agonize for minutes over a plastic doll or a tin tea set or a toy gun, but the "Anything" price was half a kyat then—it was a long time ago.

The Palladium Cinema, where Traders Hotel now stands, once had a row of narrow stalls along its front. Before an evening movie, my husband (who would become my ex and later deceased, poor man) and I would drink fresh fruit-and-milk smoothies at one kyat for each tall, frothy glass at these stalls, and then stroll toward the Sule Pagoda.

Along Bo Gyoke Aung San Road on the other side of the Palladium Cinema, by early evening the secondhand book sellers would be carefully laying out their tattered paperback editions of English novels with crumbling, yellowed pages. Some of the old books had a seal on the cover proudly saying "Home library of ...," part of a treasured collection sold off after their owner's death or by a living bibliophile who needed cash.

I still treasure the books I found there: *Gal Young Un and Other Famous Stories of the Cross Creek Country* by Marjorie Kinnan Rawlings, *Aimez-vous Brahms?* by Françoise Sagan, *Nine Stories* by J. D. Salinger, and all four books of the Alexandria Quartet by Lawrence Durrell. I remember hopping with delight right there on the sidewalk when I found the Durrell set, at five kyat each. That was a rather high price for me at the time, but I was determined to have them even if it wiped out my next day's market money.

My husband was furious that I behaved like "a hooligan, jumping up and down in public," relenting only when he saw how happy I was. I read and reread these books for years, keeping the pages together with tape.

My Yangon life was at its most intense from the 1960s to the 1990s, when I was a painter until I became too involved with my writing to continue. In the poverty of the Socialist economy there were absolutely no ready-primed canvases to be had so we primed our own. The first coating was a thin layer of thin rice paste. I would stand the bare canvases, about twenty for each batch, in a row in the garden. As I went down the row carefully applying this starchy liquid, my dog would often be right behind me, licking it off.

For annual shows I would paint from morning until night, stopping only for a quick bite. At times I would find my fingers so stiff I could not flex them at all, not even to pick up and hold a brush. I would then tie a brush into my fist with a strip of rag and not untie it until I was done for the day, using the same brush over and over again, washing it in turpentine each time I chose another color.

Another intense period was the two years and nine months I spent in Yangon's Insein Prison, but that was a different and extremely interesting type of intensity.

One evening a few years ago, after a dinner of puffy poori and potato curry with a friend at our favorite Indian eatery, I stopped to look at one of the stalls in downtown Yangon that sells "Anything for Five Hundred." To my delight I spotted a small compass.

For someone with a disposition like mine, I was sure this was bound to come in handy someday.

Later I decided to float down the Ayeyarwaddy River from its confluence to where it flows into the sea. Since rivers go only in one direction and because I would be traveling by boats navigated by someone else, I would not need my compass, I thought.

I was wrong.

PART I
Birthplace of the Ayeyarwaddy

CHAPTER ONE

Dancing at the Manau

My first steps toward a ride down the thirteen hundred-mile Ayeyarwaddy River began with a roll of drums, although not at all on my account. It was at a celebration on the northern tip of Myanmar and issued from great twenty-foot-long drums beaten by well-muscled Kachin men.

"There's going to be a major Kachin Manau festival in Myit-kyina, right after Christmas," said Ko Sonny Nyein. A sculptor and painter, Ko Sonny and I go way back, at least twenty-five years, when we first met as members of the Peacock Gallery in Yangon.

Ko Sonny and his wife Amy are quiet and conservative by nature and hover over me like guardian angels—Ko Sonny rather like a tubby winged one. Both of them are constantly appalled at the risks I take in traveling alone, although it is very safe to travel in my country, and as a woman in my very mature years, I face no flirty harassment.

I knew that it was with grave misgivings that he invited me on this trip. Myitkyina is a civilized town in the Kachin State, full of well-behaved Christians and Buddhists, but Ko Sonny worries needlessly and all the time. Besides, he knows I like to veer off into unplanned routes.

The Kachin is one of the largest ethnic groups in Myanmar, living in the northeast of the country among wide plains and mountains. Their land has jungles, ice-capped mountains, and rivers. It produces gold and the best jade in the world, the Imperial Jade of the translucent grass-green so prized by the Chinese as a stone of honor and good fortune. This jade is found in astonishing abundance; a seventy-foot-long massive boulder was found in 2001 on New Year's Day, forty feet underground. The mining company willingly handed it over to our country, saying something of this immensity should be handled by the national government.

I could not imagine what I would have carved out of this, given a chance—six billion pairs of earrings, maybe—but more likely the very first item that will be carved from it will be a Buddha image, bet you anything. As a Buddhist country of deep beliefs, Myanmar has tens of thousands of pagodas of every size dotted all over the country and uncountable Buddha images, with new ones being made every hour.

The people of the Kachin State also make woven cloth in red and black patterns, cane ware, and, most important to me, great food. Their food may be an acquired taste for Westerners, but for Myanmar palates, authentic Kachin noodles with pickled bamboo shoots or rice-tofu salad swimming in gravy or minced pork wrapped in banana leaves are gourmet meals which are not available in Yangon. They also have the sweetest pineapples and a nut called nga pauk which is creamier than the best pistachios. A famous French restaurant in Yangon, Le Planteur, drizzles nga pauk oil in a circle around their filet mignon.

Another fruit that I have not found anywhere else but in the Kachin State is the star apple, and people from other countries whom I have asked do not know it at all. It has a shiny, thin rind which is either maroon or green in color, and is the size of an apple. The inside is full of white, creamy, custardy flesh, with five small black seeds, and is said to be full of nicotine. I could eat twenty at a sitting, halving them with the penknife that I always carry with me and scooping out the flesh with a spoon which—needless to say—I always have on hand as well. Since I gave up smoking years ago, I feel I can afford to indulge in nicotine in this other form.

The Manau is a Kachin celebration for a good harvest or for the New Year, a public affair where clans gather. This one, to be held in Myitkyina over eight days starting on December 26, 2001, was on a scale that had not been seen for a hundred years. It would be a gathering of the eleven Kachin ethnic groups, the Jinghpaw, Trone, Dalaung, Guari, Hkahku, Duleng, Maru, Rawang, Lashi, Arsi and Lisu, and their subtribes, with other neighboring groups such as the Shan, Pa-O, and Palaung invited as well. Even tribes from across the border in China would attend, and the news went to Kachin ethnic groups living in the United States, Canada, and other countries overseas.

This festival was announced in September, and we were determined to go, with plans to leave on December 23. Most annoyingly, just one airline flew to this corner of the country so it would be hard to get flights that would bring us home; we could only book one-way flights from Yangon. Lucky me—I was not planning on flying back if I could help it.

By the morning of the twenty-fifth I was still sitting in my flat, fuming as I waited for tickets. It seemed that even one-way tickets from Yangon were difficult to obtain. All the flights were full and, since seats could not be booked until one day beforehand, and since priority was given to VIPs or foreigners who needed to connect with outgoing planes, locals were usually held over in a long waiting line. All this fuss for a few days' stay in Myitkyina, I thought, growing desperate.

Confident that I would leave on the twenty-third, I had airily refused all Christmas invitations, so I found myself on the twenty-fourth twiddling my thumbs and watching Korean TV soaps while others were out partridging in pear trees. I scowled at the screen, unsympathetic toward the pretty Korean brides harassed by their in-laws. I was in a foul, decidedly un-Christmassy mood.

By the afternoon of the twenty-fifth I had started to unravel and unpack, throwing things all over the carpet. I would stay locked in my flat, I decided, reading trashy novels and doing nothing. I began to look forward to this silly but restful indolence, a form of holiday I had not enjoyed for at least a year.

Ko Sonny called that evening.

"We have tickets for tomorrow. Do you still want to come? Are you ready?"

Do I ever. Am I ever.

While I was waiting for Ko Sonny to pick me up the next morning, the phone rang. It was my "adopted" son Kyaw Thura wishing me a Merry Christmas and checking to see if I was hung over. We had met many years ago under strange circumstances—i.e., politics and Insein Prison—and each had liked the way the other handled it, with equal aplomb. With mischief, even. After that event blew over, we had sort of "adopted" each other as we seemed cut from the same cloth.

Kyaw is the protective sort and feels strongly that his "mom" should not be allowed to gallivant alone all over the country, or in the company of men who are not relatives, so unless caught in the act I never tell him beforehand when I plan a trip. It would not do to tell him that I was just about to go to Myitkyina to drink and dance at a Kachin festival. He knows I love rice wine fermenting in pots, ever since he once caught sight of me at a party clutching one of those pots, not letting anyone else near it.

We chatted about Christmas parties he had been to the previous day, and he sounded pleased that for once I stayed home. I did not tell him why. Then I heard the horn of Ko Sonny's car.

"Oops, someone at the door," I said, "Gotta go, sweetie. I'll call you later. Take care."

The Ayeyarwaddy River starts a few miles north of Myitkyina, at the confluence of the Mai Kha and Mali Kha rivers. I had always wanted to float down the Ayeyarwaddy on canoes, rafts, barges, or steamers, but so far had only managed a trip from Bhamo to Mandalay to Bagan on a series of passenger boats. After attending the Manau, I had vague hopes of traveling all the way down the river, or at least boating through the infamous First Defile, one of the Ayeyarwaddy's most perilous and rock-filled gorges.

I have a penchant for getting lost but I was reassured by knowing that I could only go in one direction when floating downstream. I was sure all would be well as long as I had no need to swim during any part of my voyage. Wisely enough I did not intend to disclose my plans to my companions until our plane was safely aloft—or even much later.

We landed in the afternoon. The festivities had officially opened that morning, with speeches by dignitaries and some dancing. We had unfortunately—or perhaps fortunately—missed all that.

We settled into the one hotel that offered hot showers, albeit only in the evenings when the electricity came on. I was in a room the size of a large closet, but felt lucky that we did not have to sleep under the trees since every hostelry was packed with visitors.

The phone rang; it was a light plastic thing with a heavy cord, and I managed to upend the whole apparatus onto the floor before I put the receiver to my ear.

"Did you break something, already?" Ko Sonny asked anxiously. "Let's go out to lunch in twenty minutes. We need to plan."

We went to a restaurant run by seven strapping young Lisu women and their mother, a woman even taller than they, whose second husband was thin and mild-mannered. His stepdaughters all seemed very fond of him, but you hardly noticed him when the shop was filled with those Amazons.

Ko Maung Maung Latt ordered a variety of dishes, but when they came, they all looked the same: chunks of meat with tomatoes and onions. Luckily they tasted different, and the sun-ripened tomatoes were incredibly sweet. As we ate, we discussed our work plan for that afternoon and the succeeding days:

1. Get into the circular enclosure where the dances were held.
2. Each do our own thing, i.e., they would take photos, I would take notes.
3. Meet up at the hotel afterward.

That was exactly the type of teamwork I like: Do whatever you have to do on your own, don't wait around for each other, do meet up for meals. Discussion over in half a minute, we tucked in until we nearly burst. Back at the hotel, I fell asleep until they called again to wake me in time to go to the festival, at which point I dropped the phone again. I wondered if I should buy some superglue, just in case I broke this thing.

We hired a three-wheeled vehicle much like Thailand's tuk-tuks, but with curtains. I felt like an elderly Chinese bride escorted by two large bodyguards as we chugged our way to the fairgrounds.

I had seen photos of the Manau totem poles, but I nearly toppled out of the tuk-tuk in surprise when I saw them in real life. They towered over the fields, beautifully painted in traditional patterns of black and red over white. They were constructed out of molded concrete so that they would last for years and were of an overpoweringly majestic size.

I walked around the fairgrounds, almost tripping over people as I stared at the different costumes. The Putao Lisu ladies wore neat turbans, full gathered skirts of blue stripes on white, and sashes of polished shells. The Myitkyina Lisu had more colorful headdresses, with silver chains dangling from their turbans and hanging over their brows. Their dresses were long with finely embroidered designs at their hems.

The Jinghpaw wore red wool skirts and black velvet jackets decorated with silver ornaments. The patterns on the skirts were woven in yellow, green, and black wool that stood out against the red, and they wore turbans of the same colors. Ko Sonny was taking photos of the fabric designs and I spotted him crouched to the ground, hind end in the air, as he shot a pair of intricately woven leggings.

Dancers were already beginning to form two long lines. The leading men were dressed in long robes of embroidered satin. They wore hats on which sprouted high peacock feathers that trembled in the breeze, each with a hornbill's beak tucked somewhere in this splendid display. They held swords in each of their two hands. Those who followed them were dressed in less ornate costumes, the men in wide pants and wide-sleeved shirts with scarves around their heads, the women in their colorful clothing.

Music blared from the base of the totem poles, which were right in the center of the field. Some photographers were already inside the enclosure, so we quickly hopped into the ring and trotted across. I made straight for the drums that I knew would be on the other side.

Sure enough, there were the two long drums and three wooden stands, each holding five gongs. Two men at the end of each drum and one man for each set of gongs made up the musicians. An elderly man stood on a concrete planter, conducting with hands that looked as graceful as flying birds. The music was simple, just the constant beat of drums and gongs, but somehow I did not find it monotonous. Someone sang from the other side of the totem poles, his wailing tones amplified over the field.

The dancers filed in slow step, heading straight for the totem poles. Three times they bowed, backed off, then returned to bow again. The two lines, each made up of about two hundred people, separated and, still in slow step, marched around the perimeter of the enclosure.

As these lines began weaving in and out, twisting into intricate circles like thin, colorful dragons writhing in the sea, the dance became exhilarating to watch. The drums thumped giant heartbeats. Dancers were in single file, much like a conga line but without touching. The men carrying swords held them upright in one hand while turning their wrists in and out.

I sat on the concrete-covered floor next to the gongs in a bit of shade offered by an old packing crate. I longed to beat one of the drums at least once, but unsure if tribal laws prohibited women touching the instruments, I thought I should not even suggest it.

The master of ceremonies at the microphone invited the audience to join in; this was a freestyle dance, not the competition which would come later. Some of the photographers joined in, shaking their booties most ungracefully. One whom I knew called me to join the dancers but I shouted back that I'd rather play the drums. He rolled his eyes as he danced away, swaying his ample hips. That woman always wants to do what is absolutely never any of her business, I could almost read in a balloon over his head.

Suddenly I noticed a group of elderly ladies who were somewhere in their sixties, dressed in dark purple longyi, white jackets, and turbans of a matching shade of purple, tied in jaunty points.

Other women danced by rather demurely, holding their hands in the air and turning their wrists in and out. But the ladies in rakish purple turbans swayed like graceful palm trees, swooping sideways from the waist, their arms stretched out and fingers fluttering in the air like butterflies. I jumped up to take their photo, and then I chased them all over the field just to watch them.

They were beautiful. They knew it too; they looked at me out of the corner of their eyes and smiled smugly as I skipped after them. I felt like a pregnant rhino running alongside elegant antelopes.

The sun began to set. The slanting rays cast the dancers' shadows in long lines on the floor, dark moving shapes that wove in and out, now here, now there, running in dizzying patterns. It was visual rhythm backed by the heavy tones of the drum and accented by the sweeter notes of the gongs. I have never felt so alive in my life; I could feel my blood pounding in every vein in my body.

At dinner later that night, again at the shop of the Seven Sisters, I felt anything but alive. I longed to gobble my food and put my head down for a nap while my colleagues finished their leisurely meal. The glint in Ko Sonny's eye, however, when I threatened to rest my head on the table told me that I could not push the limits of acceptable public behavior. Besides, their friend Ko Pauk had joined us to give advice on how to plan trips farther afield, and I could not disgrace my companions. So I propped my chin up with my hands and hoped that I would not fall face-down into the vegetables.

Ko Pauk, round of face, thick of eyebrows, and a confirmed bachelor, knew the pretty Seven Sisters well and they knew him—both parties were famous in the region. He kept whispering to us that my, my, my, their food must be special, look at how huge these girls are. After asking a waiter, I found out that of the seven sisters, only two eligible girls remained. We teased Ko Pauk that he'd better move fast, and he looked both eager and terrified at the prospect of making a move on one of these Lisu beauties.

My colleagues wanted to get a shot of the confluence from above, so the Ayeyarwaddy and its two parent rivers would be in one frame. A grainy amateur photo on an old calendar hanging

nearby showed it could be done, but from where was it taken? Ko Pauk said it looked as though it had been shot from a nearby hilltop, where an army camp was situated. We planned to go there the day after next and asked that he come with us to negotiate permission from the camp, as we were sure that anyone within a radius of fifty miles would know him well. It would not be too wise, we knew, for strangers carrying cameras to creep up on an army camp.

Unfortunately, Ko Pauk had other plans, so we would be on our own. Ko Sonny knows I hate hills, mountains, or even stairs, and he gleefully insisted that I come up to the camp with them.

"No way," I said. "No climbing for me. I'm staying by the river to eat grilled fish." There was a row of tea shops on the banks at the confluence, where fresh fish were grilled over charcoal.

But I had more than grilled fish on my mind. I let them finish their meal in unsuspecting peace as I sleepily plotted and planned.

CHAPTER TWO
Witchery of Gold

I was up and ready to go in a few minutes the next morning, since I am not the thanakha aficionado that most of the women in my country are. Thanakha is a tree with thick, fragrant bark that is ground on a circular stone with water. The resulting creamy paste is applied as makeup and sunscreen, and girls and children wear patches of it on their cheeks. I love its fragrance but usually make do with a bottled version—at home or while traveling—two shakes, a quick rub all over my face, and I'm done.

(You'd have to see the others to believe how they do it. They bring along small stone slabs and short pieces of thanakha to use when they travel, and if they go to thanakha country, they bring back enough logs to build a cabin.)

Walking to the fairgrounds after the usual disgusting hotel breakfast—coffee as thin as cow piss, toast like Styrofoam with margarine like lard, and boiled eggs—we came upon some women selling oranges and grapefruit by the road. Ko Pauk had met up with us at the hotel so he came along, reminiscing with Ko Maung Maung Latt about their schoolboy mischief as they walked, poking each other in the ribs and chuckling.

The women selling oranges also had cups made of bamboo with neatly woven handles, and I immediately bought ten. I spied what we call "Washington fruit," grapefruit-sized oranges. I had never tasted one so I bought three to eat later, along with some "rose oranges," the juiciest and sweetest I have ever eaten, small with thin red skin. Ko Pauk bought tiny marble-sized oranges and handed out some to us. "Eat the whole thing," he said. Rather apprehensively, I popped one into my mouth, and chewed. It was very orangey and pulpy, not juicy, and refreshingly delicious. Immediately I asked him for more.

I was not behaving in an acceptable ladylike manner, gobbling orange after orange as we walked along. Ko Pauk gave me alarmed glances when he saw the amount I was putting away, but after a while he relaxed and treated me like one of the guys. A lady would have walked decorously by their side and would not have eaten while walking in the street, something my brother has been telling me for years.

Once we arrived at the fairgrounds, we went in different directions. I headed off toward the far edge where there were a few craft displays because I particularly wanted to see the gyat khote, or strap weaving.

The women were weaving red wool and purple thread into black weft. Their finished product was thickly woven cloth ornamented with small, detailed designs and fashioned into shoulder bags, belts, and turbans.

People milled around me, excitedly exclaiming over the exhibits. They were neither tourists nor visitors from the capital but tribes gathered here for this clan meeting, and parts of the life of this village were as new to them as they were to me. We even peeked into stalls made of leaves where na'nauk were chewing the walls. These are stout bovines, also called mithun, bigger than buffaloes or cows, with meaty shoulders and short fur in white and dark brown patches. They are prized possessions and a culinary delicacy—cooked, of course—at feasts.

Sighing about the heavy black stone pots on display that I longed to buy, I wandered out toward the entrance, thinking I would scrounge for food. I had seen roadside stalls farther away, some a mere hand's span off the dusty ground, the sort of places I am always willing to patronize. Blessed with a cast-iron stomach and an unsqueamish state of mind, I can dine with delight at any dust or fly-covered eatery.

As I neared the entrance to the fairgrounds, I saw a white-uniformed brass band come proudly marching and playing into the field. The drum major twirled his baton, chest puffed out like a rooster.

I stood aside to let them pass, delighted at their sight and sound. After they had gone in, yet another brass band marched in, playing some vaguely Chinese-sounding tune, not martial music as the other one did. Trumpets blared and cymbals clashed as I walked backward in front of this band, taking photos. Their leader held a sword upright in his right hand and had a peacock feather pinned to the front and center of his turban.

Suddenly I was aware of martial music coming from just behind my back. I froze and looked over my shoulder; the other band had made a U-turn and was heading back toward us on this narrow lane. I jumped aside hastily, thinking I might get caught between a sword and a twirling baton. I stood and watched in fascination as the two bands neared each other, playing different tunes. When they were about five feet apart on the narrow brick path they stood marching in place, still playing, staring at each other over bulging cheeks as they blew. I wondered who would give ground in this musical Mexican standoff and happily squatted on the ground to see this out for as long as it might take.

After some minutes, the drum major of the first band had enough. He called a stop to his musicians, who ceased playing one by one, the notes dropping like wet laundry falling off the line. Then he marched off in lone dignity. His band was left standing at ease but looking anything but, blocking the path of the other group which was still vigorously playing. Then the second band marched forward slowly and cautiously, playing loudly (if by now with a few discordant notes), whereupon the first one broke ranks and hastily stepped aside. I felt disappointed; I was hoping for the contest to end with some broken heads—or at least broken drums—but then, many of my countrymen have gentler natures than I.

Once back on the road I saw a stove on the ground where a woman was heating khaw-pote, cakes of cooked and mashed black sticky rice which have been dried in the sun and are then grilled before serving. A few turns over an open fire makes them warm and soft. Eaten with either sugar or pounded sesame, they are a filling, delicious snack, and I had several.

I chewed away happily, standing by the pavement, staring at the vendors and the people. There were a lot of noodle stalls, even one perched on a trishaw. A vendor had a tub of ice cream on a trolley and a bunch of balloons tied to the handle, which got the kids to come to him one way or the other.

A big tea shop had a cloth sign saying "Christmas Hamburgers." Hating hamburgers even more than I loathe chicken curry, I shuddered and turned my back.

While wandering in the fairgrounds, I came across Ko Pauk talking to a Lisu lady whom he introduced as Daw Ar Wu Mee, a teacher. I know a young Lisu whose father, a Baptist pastor, lived in a village near Myitkyina, so I asked if she knew either the Reverend John or his son Oliver, who now taught at a seminary in Pyin Oo Lwin.

"Yes, indeed, he was my student," she said, delighted. "He's very special."

I agreed. I came to know Oliver through mutual friends from Britain who met him when they were holidaying in Mandalay in 1992. While sitting at a corner shop eating fried wontons, Vicky and her mother heard a voice behind them asking in impeccable, courtly English: "Might I know your names? And where do you hail from? This is my first time in Mandalay and you are the first foreigners I have met."

"We turned around," Vicky told me years later, "and there was this very young boy wanting to practice his English, which he had no need to, since he spoke it perfectly."

He was actually about seventeen at the time, but has always looked younger than his years, so let's say he then looked as though he were ten. He had learned English from an Allied soldier who had stayed behind in a village near Myitkyina after World War II. (All over Myanmar there were men like this from different countries, so assimilated into the local life that the community no longer considered them "foreign.") Vicky, her mother, and Oliver talked for two hours and have been firm friends ever since.

At lunch, my comrades and I talked over what we had seen that morning. Speaking about other ethnic groups in our country, Ko Sonny and Ko Maung Maung Latt told me about the Naga New Year they had once attended.

The Naga tribes live in the northwest part of Myanmar, on the Indian border. Their New Year celebrations had been held in a very remote place, and I had decided not to go, learning, incorrectly as it turned out, that I might have to walk fifty miles.

The Naga dances have more complicated steps than the dances we had just seen, Ko Maung Maung Latt told me.

"As they danced in long rows," he said to us, waving his arms enthusiastically over the spicy curries, "from one end of the line to the other, they each in turn made the *trr trr* sounds with their tongues"—here he demonstrated verbally—"while the guys at the other far end went *oomph, oomph*. The sound traveled along the lines to pass at the center, then faded in the distance, and there I was right in the middle with my camera—it was a truly beautiful stereo effect."

He made a few more repeats of the *trr trr-oomph oomphs,* enjoying himself hugely. I writhed with envy.

Later on in my room, I tried to make the same sounds, both the *trr trr* and the *oomph,* but failed miserably. Much as I tried, with increasing tongue fatigue, I could not make the whirring sound Ko Maung Maung Latt had made.

That night, I discreetly inquired at the desk about the possibility of taking a boat from Myitkyina down to Bhamo, and oh joy joy joy, I found out that an express ferry service had been set up just a few weeks ago. The hotel would send someone to purchase a ticket for me right away, to ensure I would have a good seat. I pranced like a frisky goat as I relayed the news to Ko Sonny in the lobby.

Aghast at my news that I would not fly back with them and equally aghast at my scandalous prancing in public, he reminded me that the First Defile through which I would pass is notoriously dangerous.

"Never mind. If anything happens to me, my lawyer has my Last Will and Testament," I told him blithely. "Be sure to cremate me."

He went pale; it is not good form to speak aloud of omens of ill fortune such as possible death.

"*Phlat! Phlat!* Don't say such things," he spat out the sounds to drive away hovering ill luck, waving his hands in the air. "You'll be all right, and we will see each other in Yangon." This last he said loudly, and with firm conviction, to let the hovering Fates know that he would not stand any nonsense from them.

I beamed at him; one battle had been avoided. In the shock of the moment, he accepted easily that I would leave them literally high and dry.

They planned to fly home to celebrate the New Year with their families. I, without an immediate family, was free of personal encumbrances and could float down the river I love.

That night, as I snuggled in bed under the heavy woolen blanket, I thought with delight of the next day's trip to Myit Hson, the confluence. We would leave at 6 a.m. sharp to get good morning light for photographs by the time we arrived there one and a half hours later.

Unable to sleep, I thought about the time two years ago, almost exactly to the day, when I had come here with just one thing in mind: to get a good sunrise photo of the confluence.

It was December and I had flown to Myitkyina with my young artist friend Sandar Khine, a stolid, silent young lady as dependable as a personal dragon. On arrival at the airport we had hired a van, telling the driver that we would go straight to the confluence and spend the night there.

This is something even people from Myitkyina would not do; they might go for picnics, but few would want to stay the night there. By the time we declared our intentions, we were already sitting in the car. Short of pulling us out physically, the driver could do nothing, and touching us would get him into deep trouble. (In my country it's a criminal offense to even grab a woman's hand without her consent. Liable to six months in jail, you guys, remember that.)

He scratched his head and said nobody ever spent the night at the confluence, then warned us about kidnappers, bandits, ghosts, and insurgents. We said never mind, we could deal with them, let's go let's go let's go, and by the way, do you have a blanket you can lend us? He said no, which was fine with us; we had brought woollies in which we could sleep. The van was big enough for two of us; with the windows closed it would be cozy, and the driver could sleep in one of the nearby restaurants.

On our way, with the driver looking very glum, we came across two elephants transporting goods with their oozi, or handlers, perched on their necks. They were trotting along at a brisk pace. Screeching like a peahen, I told our driver to stop and, jumping out of the car, I ran after the beasts of burden, begging the oozi to please please pose for a photo. They very nicely halted their charges, which turned around and eyed me with annoyed looks. I clicked away for a few seconds, and could see the elephants practically tapping their feet with impatience. I finally straightened up and waved, whereupon they turned around so quickly that their tails swung like bell ropes. I could just imagine them saying to each other, "We're late! We're so late! That stupid moron of a woman has no idea of time … "

Our driver easily found accommodations at a tea shop whose owner he knew well, much to our collective relief. He had looked very near tears as he parked the car.

Sandar and I walked to the riverbank down a steep incline. The water's edge was covered for yards inland with round river stones. The water was clear, clean, and icy cold. We cupped our hands to drink deeply; we were not thirsty, but a legend goes that if you want to come back here, you must drink from the river. We stood there for long minutes, silent, awed by the majesty of the landscape.

Spotting a boat, we walked over to ask if it could take us up the river. The boatman was reluctant.

"Not up the Mali Kha," he said finally. "Dangerous. If you go up the Mai Kha, I can take you."

We agreed on a price and a change of rivers and were on his boat in a matter of minutes.

In the afternoon's golden sunlight, the wide and shallow river sparkled. The sound of the swift-flowing waters accompanied our boat as it sped upriver. We stopped at a flat bank lined with small stones and Sandar and I kept exclaiming over the pretty colored ones we found, picking them up, dropping some reluctantly, and clutching the ones we could not bear to leave behind. After several delirious moments, our pockets heavy with loot, we went our way again and came upon people panning for gold.

Some men had diesel pumps running, which poured water and silt from thick pipes onto a narrow runaway covered with what I thought was rusty metal mesh but turned out to be dried inner stems of banana trees, cut lengthwise. Any gold particles heavier than sand would be caught between the neat squares of nature's mesh, which is then burned to retrieve the gold.

A sunburned woman with a baby tied to her back was using a round wooden tray to pan for gold. As she expertly swirled the water out, I caught glints of the precious metal in the blackish sand. She made enough for a steady income, she told us, but the glint in her eyes revealed her hopes of hitting the jackpot. She recounted a story she heard of "someone farther up" finding lumps as big as peanuts in a single day.

We arrived back at the confluence just as the sun was setting; I got a few shots of the sun, which sank all too quickly behind the hill of In Khaing Bon.

Night fell as rapidly. Sandar and I went looking for food and found large fish grilled to perfection, wedged between split bamboo. After a dinner of boiled rice, the fish, and fried eggs offered by the food shop girls, who were round-eyed at our presence, we sat drinking hot green tea under the dim light of two candles.

We were not the only overnight guests there. There were three young men in shabby khaki uniforms, enjoying some rum after their meal at the next table. All the other shops had closed down for the night, deserted and locked tight, with the shopkeepers living in a village about a mile away.

Sandar and I studiously avoided looking at the men, whom we assumed were drunk. It was safer not to make eye contact with drinking men, especially at night. Our driver nodded sleepily at another table. The girls of our restaurant had all gone home. Except for the light from our two candles, it was completely dark and eerily silent. Distantly we could hear the faint chuckles of Mai Kha.

One of the men came over to our table, glass in his hand. We tensed, prepared for unpleasantness.

"Good evening, Aunty," he said politely, not a trace of drink in his soft voice. "The boatman told me you are interested in the gold seekers. I am going to pan for gold farther up the Mali Kha, with my friends."

By his tone of voice and his polite bow, I knew we had found a gentleman.

"Sit down!" I said immediately. "Yes, I'd like to know about you and your work. Where are you from?"

Sandar relaxed and smiled in relief.

He drew up a chair and sat a little away from us, not at our table. This showed his good manners because Sandar, a pretty young woman his age, was a complete stranger to him and it would not be gentlemanly behavior for a man to be friendly with a woman he didn't know. But because I was from an older generation, it was all right for him to talk to me.

Without much prodding he told his story.

"I was a soldier from Khun Sa's Mong Tai Army, Aunty," he said. "I lost my parents a long time ago. After he surrendered to the government, we were disbanded, and I came to make my fortune!" He laughed gently at himself. Khun Sa, the famous drug lord, had surrendered earlier that year, 1998.

I could not help asking if he himself did any drugs while working for a drug lord.

"No, I would have been punished severely, I didn't dare," he said. "He gave two warnings and the third was death."

I immediately changed the topic to gold. Better not to delve too deep into the management methods of drug dealers, I thought, considering the time, company, and place we were in.

"This is my second time here," he said. "Way up north, miles up the Mali Kha, there's a place called Shwe Hmaw. My friends and I will work together, share and share alike. See, we've got our supplies here"—he gestured toward a pile in a dark corner—"rice, oil, medicine, more tools."

I asked if he had struck it rich.

"Not yet," he smiled, hope in his voice. "But I heard of nuggets the size of peanuts that someone ... "

Shwe Hmaw, so aptly named, "Witchery of Gold."

We talked about his plans for a while. He politely addressed his remarks to me, and Sandar and I both thought him a most well-mannered chap. It turned late, I wished him good fortune, and then we women climbed into our van to pass the night shivering and sleepless in the cold, even in our woollies. The young men slept near a driftwood bonfire under the branches of a magnificent Nyaung Peinné tree.

The tree spread long, leafy limbs over the incline that sloped down to the sandy banks. To encircle its trunk would take five men, arms reaching out to each other. Even the vine-like roots falling from the limbs were as thick as trees.

When we got up the next morning the men were gone; we had heard their boat chugging away before sunrise. Actually the morning was cloudy, so there was no sunrise. We drove back to Myitkyina, defeated in the quest to photograph the sun rising over the newborn river. Next day we took a ten-hour truck ride to Bhamo through spectacular mountains, rivulets, and jungles. From there we took a boat to Mandalay, each of us with a dozen river stones in our backpack.

Now, two years later, it was up to my colleagues to get the photos. Tomorrow at the confluence I could concentrate on eating fish while learning if I could come down the river from there to Myitkyina. I would continue my river ride from Myitkyina the day after next; I had the express ferry ticket safe in my bag. Plotting in my warm hotel bed, I wriggled my toes in ecstasy. I could hardly wait for the next morning.

CHAPTER THREE
Birth of a River

A crocodile wife tells her crocodile husband in a Myanmar fairy tale that if she cannot have the heart of a monkey for dinner, she will surely die. The husband obligingly catches a monkey, who tells his captor that he does not keep his heart in his body; he keeps it on a treetop. You can guess how the story ends, and if any crocodile should ever ask me where I keep my heart I shall say, "At the birthplace of the Ayeyarwaddy." When I die I am determined to hang around that place as a ghost.

I had asked Ko Sonny to call my room as soon as he woke up, as I had not brought my alarm clock and was not sure if the front desk could handle a pre-dawn wake-up call.

During the night, waking up with a raging thirst I had grabbed a can of icy-cold orange drink out of the minibar, and had gulped down the contents without opening my eyes. When the phone rang to wake me, I reached out and swept not only it, but also the (fortunately) empty can, to the floor. Ko Sonny said calling me was beginning to hurt his ears.

He asked worriedly if he should stay behind to get shots of the balloonists from Switzerland who would arrive later in the morning to land on the dance arena, but I argued that it would be easy to get copies of this shot from one of the many photographers waiting to capture it.

"Why wait around and miss the chance to climb a really steep hill?" I asked him. He did not sound overjoyed at the prospect.

We all decided to pass up the cow-piss coffee. Our taxi sped on the dark road that was jarringly rocky once we were out of the town limits. Fortunately, the car was one of the hardy Toyota station wagons that are the modern-day mules of the hills.

We passed through silent villages of houses walled with tightly woven bamboo mats, their windows shuttered tight against the chilly air. As we entered one small community, a beautiful cream-colored dog that looked like an Inuit husky ran beside our car, barking furiously. The taxi driver gave a sideways look at our pursuer, hunched his shoulders, and picked up speed. I was sorry that the dog would lose the race unfairly, pitted as he was against an engine, but to our surprise he loped along easily at an equally fast clip. Only as the car left the village did he drop back, his duty of chasing out this white intruder accomplished. He gave a few farewell barks: "And don't let me see you here again."

Ko Maung Maung Latt turned to look back at him and laughed. He said the dog had turned back home, triumph showing in every hair of his upright tail.

"He was protecting his village, you know," he said, "and he drove away this white monster who dared to cross his territory."

We reached Myit Hson, the confluence, a little after seven. Ko Sonny started making inquiries about getting up the hill, mentioning Ko Pauk's name often and pointing to the amateur photo that had been printed as a calendar and was conveniently displayed in one shop. An elderly man who seemed to know the area took Ko Sonny aside.

"I know the man who took the photo. He took it from the top of that hill over there," he said, pointing to the awesome In Khaing Bon, guardian hill of the confluence. "It will take you three days to get up there, and the man who took that photo, he said he even had to climb a tree."

Poor Ko Sonny drooped like an emptied sack. Determined to get good photos, neither he nor his cousin would mind a three-day climb, but going up trees was something even I would not want to see them do. There would be few trees—let alone branches—able to support their weight, as each of them are easily over two hundred pounds. They looked dejected, their thick shoulders drooping glumly.

"However," the old man continued, "there's another place you can try, not far from the army camp. Go and explain to the officer in charge first, don't go crawling up the hillside without warning."

Energized by this encouragement, Ko Sonny and Ko Maung Maung Latt gulped down the coffee I had ordered and picked up their stuff. They grabbed a couple of biscuits from a plastic bag on the table and I noticed with joy that it was a package of hsar mont, salt cookies! As the men headed out to our taxi that would take them to a point nearest the camp, I grabbed what was left of the biscuits and asked for an extra packet. These I tucked into my bag and loped down toward the river. Hsar mont are slightly salty, dry ovals of crisp, pastrylike cookies that I love, which are made only in the Kachin State. Since they are too fragile to transport, I can rarely buy them in Yangon.

I passed under the same Nyaung Peinné tree beneath which my ex-drug-soldier acquaintance had once slept, and went down the incline toward the water.

Here I was at the confluence again. I walked to the water's edge carefully placing my feet on the uneven rocks. The water was still crystal clear and icy cold, and I drank as deeply as I did two years before. Sitting on a large stone that looked like a dinosaur's egg, I looked out over the two rivers.

The round stones reminded me of the ones placed on pagoda platforms as wishing stones. I wondered if the same thing would work here in this magnificent place, although it was not a pagoda.

The procedure of using the wishing stone is something I have shown often to foreign friends, and it usually freaks them out.

You must kneel before a round stone you see in front of a shrine on a pagoda. There may be two or three stones of different sizes. Heft one to see that it is neither too light, nor too heavy. Clasp your hands, try to feel reverent, and ask the mighty spirits to help you. Then ask a yes/no question: for example, shall I pass my exam? Or, will I travel to China next month? Say silently, "If the answer is yes, may the stone be as light as a feather. If it is no, then may the stone be so heavy that it sticks to the ground." It is important to state this "sticking to the ground" choice, for if you merely say, "may the stone be heavy," you may not notice the difference in weight. Lift the stone and observe the result: it will always, always favor what you want, although the prediction may not come true. Then reverse the "Ifs."

What always startles everyone who does this is that if the stone is supposed to stick to the ground according to the answer it gives you, it will stick so that you cannot lift it up completely. One point will stick to the ground as if pulled by a magnet, while you turn the stone this way and that. If it is supposed to be light, it will be easily lifted higher than when it was first hefted. Try it—and enjoy—but if you are someone with a nervous disposition, please do not go about lifting stones while praying to spirits.

I did this now with the river stone I chose for its medium weight, clasping my hands and asking the spirits of the Great River that the stone be stuck to the ground if I would one day have the chance to go all the way to the upper reaches of the Mali Kha and Mai Kha rivers. The answer was yes, yes, yes and the stone could not be lifted a single millimeter. One point of it was seemingly glued to the sand, this same stone that I had easily lifted high in the air a few seconds ago. Not like a feather, but close enough.

Is this a form of self-hypnosis? Can anyone explain this phenomenon? Seriously?

I walked toward the shops on the banks where a few boats were moored. I had to find out if I could take one to Myitkyina.

Before I could check out the transport, I was sidetracked by food. A lady carrying two baskets on a yoke set her wares down on the sand—tofu salad. She was very cleanly and neatly dressed, a pink scarf tied over her head. The baskets had four long legs each, so that they were some six inches off the ground. I went over and sat down cross-legged in the sand in front of her.

"Good baskets," I said. "Keep your food away from the sand."

"My husband wove the baskets especially for me," she said.

She had both the white, rice-based tofu and the yellow one made of chickpeas in round slabs, jellied in pans. I asked for white tofu salad, no MSG nor chilli, please.

She cut a square of tofu and began slicing it into a bowl. Suddenly the slithery blob slipped out of her hands and plopped into a cup of onion oil, splashing it all over the other bottles.

"Oh dear, such a waste," I said.

"I know, oil is so expensive, but what I really mind is getting everything so messy," she replied, cleaning the smeared bottle tops. I eyed her keenly: she looked extremely clean, with good clothes, a freshly made-up face, clean toes even, which you do not often see when you come across people selling food from yoked baskets.

I was curious about what her background might be. While I waited for her to finish cleaning up, I spied some chunks of dark red meat on a plate. It was dried and deep-fried wild boar.

"It's a bit hard," she said as I started nibbling at a piece. "Mind your teeth."

It was rather delicious, but the flavor was damaged by the harsh treatment of the sun and hot oil. Fresh-cooked boar would have tasted much better; this pre-dried version was indeed hard. As I chewed, I put out a few feeler questions in a very uninterested voice as if I were merely making conversation out of bored politeness, so as not to scare her off.

Daw Mya Kyi said she was one of the descendants of Prince Nyaung Yan, and that the clan, by now in the thousands, is still close-knit. Family members are all over the country and they can get help or support as needed from each other.

Prince Nyaung Yan was a son of King Mindon, the second-to-last monarch of Myanmar. When this old king was dying in 1878, Nyaung Yan and his brother Nyaung Oke, of all the numerous princes and princesses who had been caught up in the intrigue for the throne, were the only two who escaped slaughter.

Their half-brother Thibaw was crowned king after Mindon's death due to the manipulations of his mother-in-law, the dowager queen Hsin Byu Mashin. This cold-blooded queen, in cahoots with the ministers, had been responsible for the murders of many of Thibaw's rivals. Without a son of her own, she was ambitious for her daughter to be chief queen, a rank she herself wanted but could not get.

Both she and her daughter had been obsessed with rank and power. Queen Hsin Byu Mashin's own mother had been a chief queen but was of common stock, much despised and ultimately executed, and the sweetly bitchy queens and princesses would not have let her descendants forget it, you can be sure.

By murdering much of the royal family, she had cleared the path for her stepson—cum—son-in-law, who was a scholar and a reluctant monarch. It was the royal custom for half-siblings to marry in order to "keep the royal blood line pure." It is a wonder that this inbreeding among the whole dynasty did not have the majority of monarchs foaming at the mouth, but only one or two out of the eleven Konbaung kings went mad, and then only in their advanced years.

Prince Nyaung Yan had escaped to Calcutta under British rule but had died of fever in early 1885 before the Myanmar people could realize the hope that he and his men could overthrow Thibaw. His loyal followers had fled to the Shan hills when the British annexed Upper Myanmar in November 1885, but without their leader, their revolt against the British was unsuccessful.

As the British made their way up the Ayeyarwaddy River toward Mandalay, they had dressed a commoner as a prince and seated him in the prow of the ship. Then rumors were circulated that the British were bringing Prince Nyaung Yan to Mandalay to replace King Thibaw. With this news, unaware that the replacement was a fake prince, the Myanmar people along the river did not resist the British invasion. As they all knew Prince Nyaung Yan had escaped to the British-controlled Lower Myanmar, the story was easily believed. The British quickly took Upper Myanmar and exiled Thibaw and his family to India, where he died in 1916.

It may be that the Nyaung Yan royalists considered themselves part of his family, a proud claim that I understand and admire.

The tofu salad made by the prince's descendant was good, with shreds of lime leaves giving it a unique flavor. Replete, I got up, slapped the sand from my jeans, and went to the boats. Some were big, with a roofed cabin all along their length, but others looked as if they would seat at most ten. That should do, I thought.

I woke up the boatman, who was none too pleased. No, he took picnickers across the river or on short trips up the Mai Kha. He would not go to Myitkyina. A woman squatting nearby with some luggage said she was going back to her village up the Mali Kha.

"There are boats coming down from the Shwe Hmaw gold mines that pass our villages, then they go on to Myitkyina," she said to me. "They don't usually stop here unless they are dropping off someone, but you can flag one down."

Just like waiting for a bus, I thought. I was worried that the boatmen might not pay attention to a woman flapping her arms from the bank, so I sought a figure of authority. He was sitting under a lean-to, a slight young man who was in charge of this jetty.

I explained that I would like to take the boat from here to Myitkyina as long as I would arrive before the next morning. He laughed and said I would get there in less than two hours and there should be a boat coming soon. He would make sure it stopped to pick me up.

Thanking him, I headed back toward the restaurant to wait for Ko Sonny so that I could tell him I would be making my own way. If I did not do that and left before he came back, he might think I had drowned and the soft-hearted chap would run up and down the bank, wailing and beating his chest.

As I strolled along the shore where the water lapped at the stones, I noticed a few boys running toward me.

"Aunty! Aunty! Get away!" they shouted. "We're going to explode a bomb."

Bomb? I stood still, with one foot frozen in midair.

"Over there, but you'd better step back," one of them said, pointing to somewhere in the river. There was a boy standing in knee-deep water, who tossed a small bundle into the water a few yards in front of him. There was a mild explosion, as if a medium-sized firecracker had gone off, and sprays of water rose a few feet into the air.

"Are you mining for fish?" I asked the boys, daring to put my foot down at last.

They shrugged. "We'll get the smaller ones, that's all. We just like the sound of it."

They ran into the water and scooped up the stunned fish that were the size of coins and glittered like pure silver. The whole catch wouldn't feed a cat.

I went up the cliff to wait for Ko Sonny and as I went into the tea shop, two men came in carrying plastic bags on a yoke they shouldered. I saw gleaming fins and scales.

Immediately I followed them to the back of the kitchen, where they dropped the bags, took up the bottom corners, and poured out the fish like a pirate's treasure of silver.

I had never before seen fish so fresh and shining. The mouths of the smaller ones were open like rosebuds, a deep pink in the depths when the sun fell on their cheeks. I ordered the largest fish to be grilled, thinking it would be ready by the time my companions got back. I sat at a table sipping green tea and eating the hsar mont cookies, trying not to feel sorry for the fish.

Our white Toyota monster drove up in a cloud of dust and Ko Sonny and Ko Maung Maung Latt came swaggering into the shop, with wide grins on their faces. They turned on the monitor of their video so I could see the three rivers, shining in flecks of silver, framed by forests.

"Did you have to climb any trees?" I asked—needlessly, since they looked uninjured.

"No, but we had to walk over what the captain said was an old minefield, since our spot was quite far from the camp," Ko Sonny said. "Nice chap, he led the way, as he knew where it's safe to put his feet down, and we just walked in his footsteps."

Talk about taking risks. I might go down rivers but never in my life would I set one toe in a minefield.

"Promise you won't tell our wives," they warned, and I swore I wouldn't.

From their vantage point they had seen the "mine" explode in the river. They had been relieved to see me walking around afterward so they knew they were spared the bother of picking up bloody little pieces of my body to take back to Yangon.

They were ecstatic at their success, having brought back prints and slides of the two rivers flowing together to become one. With a steaming-hot grilled fish in front of them in a matter of minutes, they were two very happy men.

"Er, Ko Sonny, I think I won't drive back with you guys, I'll take the boat down to Myitkyina," I said, reaching for the fish with my bare hands. With better social graces than I, they were poking at it with chopsticks and I knew my bad manners would get me more fish than the two of them combined.

"What boat?" Ko Sonny asked suspiciously. I explained about hitching a ride.

"You're doing it again!" Ko Sonny exclaimed, dropping his chopsticks to stare at me. "You're always doing this."

"But it's so beautiful," I protested. "You should come along, too. Send the car back. You both should see this part of the river.

You won't get the chance again for a long time," I warned, playing my trump card. If one of them came with me, they would not be so annoyed and might invite me again on other trips.

Finally, Ko Sonny agreed to go with me, while Ko Maung Maung Latt would take the car back to arrange for their return tickets.

I sat bouncing gently on my chair, swinging my legs and licking my fingers, pleased that I would be starting the river ride from the very birthplace of the Ayeyarwaddy. Things are falling into place, I thought, and going far better than I had hoped.

After the fish was demolished, Ko Maung Maung Latt stood on the riverbank watching as Ko Sonny and I went down to get our ride. Just as we reached the river's edge, a boat from upstream chugged up. Luckily it stopped to let off a passenger at the jetty, so we had no need to flag it down. We walked up to it, ingratiating smiles on our faces.

"Can we come along to Myitkyina?" I asked a boy who held the boat's prow against the sand to keep it steady as a man jumped off. "Please?"

"No," he replied shortly. "We're overloaded."

I pleaded with more fervor, clutching at the side of the boat.

"Please, it's just the two of us, we've got no luggage, and we're not too heavy."

A disdainful glance at our bellies from the boy; he knew a lie when he saw the evidence.

I begged some more, not sure there would be another boat.

"Oh, let them come," said a man huddled near the prow, and the boy silently helped us on board.

We sat on someone's luggage. The other passengers, about twenty in all, were seated along the narrow length on wooden seats which were mere planks wedged in sidewise, or on plastic mats on the floor. There was no roof.

I looked at the passengers behind me. The sun glowed with

a white light and was by then very fierce, although not as hot as it would be in Yangon. Bags and baskets were wedged in tightly among the people, and behind me was a bulging plastic basket with three winter melons and a small white hen. Wrapped up in a piece of transparent pink plastic to keep its wings secured, the chicken looked as if it wore a flimsy party dress. I moved my shoulders so that my shadow would fall directly over its eyes, as the sun was brilliantly bright. I hoped it would not be cooked with the winter melons; it looked too small to make much of a meal. I imagined it growing up in a kitchen garden, ruffling its pretty white feathers and scraping importantly in the dust, becoming a pet that would lay hundreds of eggs for the family.

The man who had allowed us into the boat turned out to be the owner. He had little to say and left things much to the boy, who was the conductor, with a moneybag belted around his chest and over one shoulder and someone I thought I'd better make friends with.

I started out asking him my usual moronic questions: Oh, is that a bird? How pretty! Are there many fish? Is it always this cold on the river? Strangers usually relax when the first questions are silly. Years ago I had found out the hard way that in times of questioning it goes easier if you play the dimwit—whether you are the interrogator or the interrogated.

After we were chatting easily, I learned that the boy's name was Zaw Naung, a typical Kachin name.

"One mother, one son," he said, using the Burmese expression "A may t'khu, thar t'khu" to say he has no other family. His father passed away last year "of a lung disease."

His lips tightened as he said that. He was eighteen, but had the look of innocence about him that made it seem as if he were hardly in his teens.

His eyes lit up and he smiled to show deep dimples when he described the pine trees upstream of Mali Kha.

"They are so tall," he threw up his arms into the air, "and growing so thickly, you would think someone planted them carefully. So beautiful ... "

I asked about animals: what kinds are there? Bears? Deer? Leopards?

"All kinds," he answered firmly. At my dubious look, he said even more stoutly, "All kinds of animals." His tone suggested at the very least the presence of unicorns or the Pyinsa Rupa, a mythical creature with a body made up of parts from five different animals.

The river twisted and turned, the water that beautiful sea green we usually think only oceans have. Ko Sonny sat like a happy bear, taking pictures left and right. At one point in a narrow turn in the river we passed several pointy black boulders rising out of the blue waves, which broke against them with white foam splattering into the air. The water was a deep blue there; the current was strong and the boat wobbled. A narrow, pale cream-colored sandbank nearby was dotted with more black boulders, looking like an especially exquisite Japanese garden.

At a bend in the river, while I was looking the other way, Ko Sonny nudged me, pointing in another direction, and I nearly fell off my perch in amazement. There, rising some miles beyond the bank were two pointy high hills, and I realized I had found my brassiere.

Not my own personal bra.

When I was in San Francisco, the limousine driver who picked me up at the airport proudly pointed out their Twin Peaks. After my return, I had written about the trip, saying that the San Francisco peaks are at best a size 30A, whereas in Myanmar we have twin peaks that are known as the brassiere of a famous actress whose size was at least 36D. I had seen a photo of the marvel—the peaks of the mountain, I mean, and not the lady's—but never in real life before.

Where the river widened, the water turned a light, sparkling sea green. We passed huge black iron steam engines pumping up silt and water onto rows of mesh. They looked like the machines you see in movies of destroyed worlds.

Where people used smaller pumps, the residue silt was left in small cones. At one place, we saw several workers and yards upon yards of neat sandy cones like baby pyramids ... I hoped this group would find gold the size of peanuts ...

Apart from these dedicated treasure seekers, I saw little human presence on the river, not even a village. In some places a jungle of thick trees towered on the banks and rang with the cries of strange birds. Waterfowl sat in clusters at the shallow edges of the river, preening their feathers.

The riverbank in most places was lined with round brown stones, smaller than those at the confluence. We passed two nuns in their fluttering pink and red robes walking on the deserted bank, looking down as if they were searching for something; I think they were mesmerized by the pretty shapes and patterns of the stones. Their reflections gleamed red in the bright green of the waves, backed with the darker green of the forest. The river was like liquid jade.

We dropped off several passengers along the way and let off the boss at one stop before Myitkyina, where the boy said he also lived. It was a village called Naung Nan, and on the banks stood a dozen or so boats at various stages of construction. The smell of fresh paint overwhelmed us as we docked next to one being painted in bright red and blue.

"How much would a boat cost?" I asked Zaw Naung, all of a sudden smitten with a fierce desire to own one. I could have a little roofed space to sleep in with someone to man the engine or paddles and take me up and down the Ayeyarwaddy, but I thought it would be far beyond my means.

"All told, including engine, at the most about 600,000 kyat," said Zaw Naung. A little less than $1,000 U.S. Not really too much beyond my means.

I began to daydream about private rides on the upper reaches of the river, already seeing "my" boat in its colors: white trimmed with blue. In the middle, an open cabin with a white roof and deep blue curtains, with a thick, soft, white mattress inside and silk cushions in all colors of the rainbow. I would have a shelf to keep books, a basket to keep clothes, another one for pots and pans and food, the third for soap and mosquito repellent and lipstick. A portable stove in the prow. A roofed and comfortable seat for the boatman in the stern, since usually they have to stand out in the open. The boat would be named, of course, Mali Kha, written in curly black letters. I had everything worked out, except for what I would do with a boat in Myitkyina when I lived in Yangon ...

We landed in Myitkyina two hours after we left the confluence and took a trishaw back to town, getting off at an Indian restaurant for a late lunch. It was already afternoon and the grilled fish had dissolved long ago.

As we dropped into our seats, Ko Sonny and I grinned at each other with delight. The trip had been wonderful. We felt at peace with the world, even with the men at the next table with a TV remote in their hands, eyes riveted upon Bollywood torsos in wet saris gyrating madly to ear-splitting music.

To celebrate the magnificence of the river we had come through, I ordered expensive river prawns. Some foreigners refuse to believe that Myanmar river prawns really come out of rivers because they are so huge, some weighing a bit over ten ounces. They are usually about six inches long from head to tail, not counting the length of whiskers or the spike in the head. Local people prefer the river prawns over other varieties, as the strong currents produce muscular and chewy flesh.

What I love, what we all love, about the prawns is the red-pink-yellow lumps of creamy tomalley in the heads that we call pazun hsi or "prawn oil." Most Asian people share this preference and consider it a delicacy. Some years ago, to my horror I had discovered that Westerners throw this away but eat the black sac that we know as the stomach and which we discard.

I had once watched a European woman at a dinner hosted by her fellow countrymen eating the dry green stuff, while I dolefully poked at the prawn head lying on my plate, bereft of any sign of the pink cream—the chef had carefully scraped out every drop. Now, free from the prejudices of Western chefs, I scooped out this rich pazun hsi and piled it on my spoonful of rice. Oh, yum. We ate slowly, relishing the food, as all we had to do was to find our way back to the fair later in the afternoon.

When we were ready to return to the fairgrounds, we saw nothing of Ko Maung Maung Latt, who must have still been chasing after tickets. We took a tuk-tuk to the field where we could see the balloons moored and stationary up in the blue heights of the sky. In an instant of practicality, I worried about what would happen if one of the balloonists needed to pee. Ko Sonny began to moan about the balloon landings he had missed and I promised that I would get a print from one of the photographers.

As we walked toward the enclosure, a light grey balloon began to descend and then swooped over our heads. Ko Sonny, without moving a step, was able to capture it on his camera as it flew past the totem poles. For days afterward he told everyone he met and everyone he went out of his way to meet about this piece of luck—he had only to lift his camera without moving one inch left or right to get the perfect shot.

Suddenly we heard an excited buzz of noise and a clash of cymbals and turned to see a pink creature stalking onto the paved area, escorted by a walking orchestra of drum, flute, and cymbals. It was a Toe Naya, a creature important in the mythology of the northern part of the country. The real ones—if they had ever existed—were supposed to have horns like a deer and musk which was the most prized of perfumes. A book written on paper parabeik, or a folding manuscript, recorded in the eighteenth century that a pair of these fabulous beasts had once been presented to the Burmese king.

This one walking toward us had a white-painted wooden face, two short yellow horns, and fur made from pink plastic twine cut in lengths of about eighteen inches, doubled over and attached to his body. A man struck a pose in front of the pink-furred creature, the music started, and away they danced from one end of the arena to the other.

The creature came to life under my popping eyes as it pranced, shook its neck, scratched fleas on its shoulder with a paw, and nibbled at itches on its flanks. The movements were so lifelike that I forgot there were two men inside an object made out of pink plastic string. I wanted to go up and scratch its ears, especially when it chewed on the fleas it had caught in its teeth.

Its dance partner leaped back, stepped closer, and teased it with graceful motions. That was the kind of dancing I would love to do: swaying and stalking a pink creature as it wagged its head and hindquarters or pretended to rush its partner with its head down like a charging bull. I was almost sure, aided by my imagination and the skill of the men inside, that this was a real creature of the jungle that could pierce my body and carry me around on the delicate points of its horns.

I decided not to have dinner that night; the river prawns had made me eat two platefuls of rice, which still sat in lumps inside me. Once in my room I turned the phone upside down to check if anything was broken, then packed my bag. The bamboo cups and any unnecessary clothing I packed into a smaller bag for Ko Sonny to take back to Yangon. I would travel light.

CHAPTER FOUR

Defiled on the Ayeyarwaddy

The ferry would leave at nine, my ticket said, but in my excitement I was wide awake and up by six. I fussed over my bag, repacking everything, and then it was time for breakfast.

Ko Sonny, Ko Maung Maung Latt, and I decided to walk a few yards to a tea shop, where we each ate two fluffy, soft, buttery Indian paratas, wrapped around brown peas boiled to a tenderness that melted on your tongue and fragrant with deep-fried onions. The tea was strong and sweetened with condensed milk. I wolfed down the food enthusiastically, licking my fingers from time to time.

Afterward I forgave the hotel owner for his cow-piss coffee when he personally took charge of arranging my transportation. My friends could not come with me to the jetty, since they had to wait for various people to call them that morning.

The night before, Ko Sonny had insisted on giving me fifty thousand kyat with a long list of phone numbers of friends in the region to call if I should "get into trouble." He was not quite sure how I was going to find a phone booth on the First Defile, however.

As my companions stood in front of the hotel seeing me off, the hotel proprietor told the trishaw driver to see me safely aboard before he came back, and to pedal slowly, and to be careful of traffic—which in Myitkyina was practically nonexistent at this time of day. He spoke to the trishaw chap in a loud, firm voice that warned he would be most upset if his orders were not followed through.

As I was pedaled away I grinned widely to see the anxiety combined with annoyance on Ko Sonny's and Ko Maung Maung Latt's faces. Drat that woman, there she goes, she may get drowned dead yet and then we'll get trouble from our wives.

When we lost our way, the trishaw man pedaled up and down the riverside until we finally spotted my ride, a very slim, long boat, painted a sickly yellow-green, with seats along its length much like a bus.

There were two wooden gangplanks leading up to the boat. My trishaw driver came aboard with me, leading the way and carrying my bag. I followed on wobbly legs along the wobbly planks.

Thanking the trishaw man and tipping him well for his kindness, I placed my bag under my feet and looked around. A few passengers were climbing into the boat and looking for seats. We all walked inside the ferry with our backs bent, as the ceiling had lethal-looking iron bars running across its breadth to reinforce the roof where goods were stacked.

In front of me where the bow narrowed to a point, a row of seats on each side was placed facing away from the water. Beginning with my row, the seats faced front, four in each row. I was in the front row and had ample legroom, but the seats behind were cramped—the passengers in those rows would have to sit with their knees practically up against their chests.

I decided to look for the loo before we cast off and found it was way at the back of the upper deck. To get there, I had to climb onto the side of the ferry, grab hold of the railing, and edge along a three-inch narrow ledge, first past the bridge and then past a glassed-in private cabin with Western tourists inside. The loo had no roof and a wall that was only shoulder-high, so everyone around could see whomever was about to sit down. On the other hand, it was well ventilated—and in any case, in Myanmar we tend to ignore these sorts of difficulties, relying on modesty and good manners to ensure privacy. In the same way, we also have a strong tendency to ignore unpleasant things.

Someone clanged a large brass bell and in a few minutes we were off chugging down the Ayeyarwaddy. On one side was the

Strand Road in Myitkyina, and on the other a row of hills stacked one after the other, with colors ranging from green-blue to misty blue to light mauve, growing paler in the distance.

A bright-eyed, slim, and attractive woman in her thirties was sitting kitty-corner from me surrounded by bags and baskets of food. She had thick, scraggly eyebrows over sparkling dark eyes, and I did not have to pry too much to get her story.

As she chomped on a large bun, she told me that she lived in Bhamo and that she was going home with goods bought for her store ... all the way from China, since to buy them in Myitkyina would be more expensive. Apparently she was not taking into consideration her travel costs.

But China? I pricked my ears. I had only been to the border town of Ruili, and since then have wanted to go further inland.

"Did you go alone?" I asked in amazement. Even on business trips, women are apt to travel in groups.

"Yes, I go alone, it's quicker if I don't have to hang around waiting for others," Mar Mar Soe, or literally "Hard Hard Ruling," said. "Women spend too much time looking in mirrors, they do it endlessly."

I beamed at her. My kind of traveler.

"First I was scared to be alone, my knees actually went wobbly, but I'm used to it now. Besides, our Myanmar people are always willing to help you, wherever you run into them."

I asked her if she ever had any problems at the border.

"Oh, no, we're legally allowed to go over the border to trade, so there are a lot of us and once there I keep in touch with the other Myanmar people."

She chatted about her shop, her family, and her two kids. Her husband worked in Bhamo and looked after the children, with her mother living with them to do the cooking. When she was home, she said she liked to relax by going to the video halls, where she would watch a couple of romances in a single sitting.

"But I can only do it when my husband's away," she giggled. "He hates me watching movies, it's supposed to lead to immoral conduct." She used a common idiom that mothers and husbands use to warn us when we are caught reading novels or watching movies: "Pyet see mai!" literally meaning, "You will become decadent!"

"I just love Nandar Hlaing, Khaing Thin Kyi, and Htet Htet Moe Oo. They're so pretty! Like porcelain dolls," she sighed, naming three top movie stars.

Learning that I live in Yangon, she asked eagerly if I had ever seen any of her favorite actresses. When I told her that I once saw Htet Htet Moe Oo in Bo Gyoke Aung San Market and that Htet Htet's complexion really does look like porcelain, I rose in her esteem.

Mar Mar Soe told stories about her trips, saying she prefers the ferry to going by road, since it was more comfortable and safer.

"I was in a truck once, between Bhamo and Myitkyina," she said, "and a wheel came off while we were going at full speed. That wheel rolled away for miles. Lucky we were not on a cliff at that moment or I'd be dead."

She fell silent, and I was left undisturbed to gaze and dream. The riverbanks were bare of any trace of humans, and tall trees formed a thick curtain just beyond the sand. I could visualize young Zaw Naung's "all kinds of creatures" cavorting in this forest.

Fat brown waterfowls sat patiently in groups as if they were officials in a town meeting. A black cormorant swooped and flew away with a wriggling fish in its beak. Several miles later a whole group of these birds sat in the river shallows, their beaks upturned to the skies, looking like a conference of dignified judges in their black robes.

An elephant and his oozi on his back ambled along the river, as if they were just out for a stroll. At that point, the river was still so wide that the elephant looked tiny. Another elephant was in the river, having a bath with his oozi trying to scrub him down. The elephant was wriggling around and beating on the water with his trunk, the way that a two-year-old child does in his bath.

We passed a hill that had one side broken off into the water, the cliff sliced in a perfect vertical, like a cut cake. Below that place, there were large, black-limbed trees half-submerged in the water, their clawlike branches reaching up as if for help. I could almost hear them screaming in this frozen moment of drowning.

As we slowed down while approaching a village, I saw a farm perched on the cliff, a richly dark green pelt of grass and a sweep of tiny yellow mustard flowers sparkling in the sunlight. The thatched roof of the hut could be glimpsed in a far corner, blue smoke rising from the back ... a thick green forest behind it all, the top of the trees touched with light. I felt I was seeing the one place in the world where I might find perfect happiness. This is Shangri-la, I thought. It isn't living forever, as in the book *Lost Horizons*; it is finding contentment in a place like this.

A young man sitting on my other side had awakened and politely offered his rice to me before eating. I smiled and said thank you and took out my own steamed sticky rice cakes that he in turn declined.

We passed yet more drowning trees, and I asked him if anyone ever took them home to use as firewood. He laughed and said no, there was plenty of firewood around. Who would want to bother going into the river when you could just break off a branch? Then, giving me a glance which seemed to take in everything about me, he said that understandably the waterlogged trees would be valuable in Yangon, but not here.

I saw a plantation of very tall, grasslike plants topped with thick silvery strands that shone in the light like blonde heads. "What's that?" I pointed.

"Sugar cane," he replied. I had seen sugar cane before but

never as lush as this—and with Marilyn Monroe hair.

By early afternoon, we were nearing the First Defile and the river was beginning to narrow. As we approached Hsin Bo, "Male Elephant," Village, which is the town just before the mouth of the Defile, the scenery grew more spectacular. The water, which all along had been a clear jade green, started to have slight tinges of muddy yellow. There were high cliffs and thick forests on each side of the river with sandbanks in only a few places.

"After Hsin Bo," said Mar Mar Soe, uncurling herself, "we will go into the Kyauk Twin, 'the Rock Pit.'"

What a name, I thought, recalling stories about the jagged rocks and white foaming waters of the First Defile.

By early afternoon, we neared the entrance of the Rock Pit and I was very excited. Sensing my interest, both Mar Mar Soe and the young man, Moe Zaw, promised to point out the landmarks: the Buddha image on the left bank near the entrance, and the pagodas in the middle and near the exit.

The first was built by a group of jade miners. It was so high up on a humped back of a rock that I could not really make it out.

"Some say it was erected in gratitude for the riches they found," Mar Mar Soe explained. "Some say it was in memory of their teammates who drowned at this spot."

Both stories sounded plausible.

"This is a rich river, she gives you gold, she gives you silver," she sang, making up her own lyrics to a few bars of a love song.

The water rushed by faster and had turned completely muddy by now. The river was narrower at some places than others, going around bends almost at right angles. A hill loomed up just in front of us until I was sure we would ram into its side, but then the boat swerved just in the nick of time.

Large reddish rocks jutted out of the river like mammoths sleeping in the shallows. There was a narrow path between the rocks

through which our slim boat could pass easily. In the rainy season, or in the hot weather when the river in this part would be swollen from melted ice and snow, the muddy water level would hide the dangerous rocks. Then the water would rush with a roar of tigers, but now at the end of December, it was mild. I was a bit disappointed, but that fleeting emotion must have been pure hypocrisy. I was as alarmed as any of the others when we heard something hard scraping the bottom of our boat a few minutes later. We drew a collective breath, held it, and when we did not sink ... ker-plonk ... let it out again ... slowly ... phew.

The steep sides of the river were thick with trees as their top branches locked fingers with each other. Vines fell from great heights, entwined with droopy purple trumpet flowers or perky-faced white blossoms. In the shade cast by the cliffs, the air was icy.

We passed a grove of tall green trees that came down almost to the water's edge. At their center stood a tree straight and tall with all its branches clustered right at the top, bunched like a bouquet. The leaves were large, round, and golden-yellow. In the midst of the dark green trees, it stood out a bit higher, and with sunlight piercing the golden leaves it looked like a torch.

Moe Zaw was napping but woke up just in time to point out a whitewashed pagoda almost hidden in the grass on the top of a hill. It looked as if someone had put a lot of blue in the whitewash, with a pretty azure tinge to it. By that time we must have passed the Rock Pit, for although the river had not widened, it had fewer of the hulking boulders in the water.

Finally, as we were about to leave the Defile there was yet another landmark, a pagoda on the right bank, on the side of a cliff. The river curved and narrowed there, and the current did not seem to be flowing very strongly. But still some of the boatmen rushed from bow to stern.

I peered around but to my inexperienced eye nothing seemed

to be wrong. The channel was very narrow, but the boat seemed to be doing fine, despite making strange detours to avoid rocks or whatever lurked underneath.

The crew dashed from fore to aft and back again; all we could see of them was their feet. Some were barefooted and wearing flapping longyi, some wore jeans and canvas shoes.

I noticed one pair which was exactly the style I had been looking for, and debated whether it would be all right to grab the owner's ankle if he passed again to ask where he had bought them, but realized it might startle him enough to tip him overboard.

Once we had passed through the First Defile, the river turned placid and wide with a look of innocence, the surface smooth with only the slightest ripple. The sun darkened to a rich golden-red and began to sink. The sky turned purple, streaked with faint yellow.

As our ferry came up to the Bhamo jetty, Mar Mar Soe, Moe Zaw, and I scanned the waterfront to see if the boat to Mandalay was moored there. It came only on alternative days so if one was not leaving the next day, I would have to stay longer in Bhamo. Not that I minded too much, but I was eager to be away as soon as possible. It was Moe Zaw who spotted my next vessel, docked about a mile away from where our express would land.

"There it is, Aunty," he said. "I think you have time to get a ticket. If the cabins are sold out, just get a place in the front room. It's better than on the open decks."

The landing was steep. Some sort of steps had been cut in the sandy bank but it looked as if I could easily slip and fall back into the boat again. Huffily thinking I should have carried a walking stick, I tried to ease my bulk up the steps when I saw a hand from above reaching down to take my bag and pull me up at the same time. It was Moe Zaw. I smiled thankfully at him and clambered up.

Once we were on top of the bank, he was away with a nod, after handing my bag to a man who looked as though he was a horse-cart driver. He had a long, thin whip in his hands, wore a tattered but clean shirt, and had an open, good-natured face, beaming to show betel-stained teeth. He waved over a boy of about ten.

"Here, son," he said, handing the boy my bag, "take this bag and this Old Mother to the cart. I'll see if I can get another passenger." He turned away toward the other travelers now milling about on the road.

Old Mother? Old Mother?

I honestly value the respect my people have for age, but *Old Mother?*

I sulkily sat in the horse cart, nursing my wounded ego. The little boy sat composedly at the front, looking neither bored or sulky nor brimming with joy. His face was an exact replica of his father's, but his teeth were still nice and white and he looked very handsome. He had neat features, a very shapely pair of lips that any girl would envy, and sweeping black eyebrows like feathers. He was a very dignified little boy.

As we sat waiting, a street peddler passed by carrying a bamboo frame with little plastic cars, blowing shrill bursts on a whistle. The boy looked at him and ran his eyes over the toys, but I could see no desire to own one on this young face. He looked as if childhood games had nothing to do with him and as though he was already burdened with life.

That deluded, moronic, blind horse-cart driver came back without any passengers. If he goes around calling people Old Mothers, I thought, he is not going to get much business. At least he was fond of his son. Getting on the cart, he ruffled the boy's hair and looked at him lovingly. The boy smiled. It was good to see and I forgave the father at once.

"You should go first to talk to someone on the boat," the horse-cart driver said when I asked about the boat to Mandalay. "You can buy a sleeping space right there."

His name was Tun Tun, and his son was grandly named Yan Naing Tun, "Conquering Enemies with Brilliance." The horse was Mya Hmwe, "Emerald Fragrant" or "Fragrant Emerald." He was a reddish pony with shaggy fur and a mind of his own, I was to discover. There was nothing the least emeraldlike about him, nor was he fragrant.

Off we went down the road leading out of town to where the boat was moored. We rode along twisting streets lined with the shady Kokko, "rain," trees, tall and beautiful with graceful, nearly black trunks and branches, their leaves a thick, deep green.

Our cart went slowly. It seemed as if it hardly moved, although the horse's steps were quick enough. Maybe, I thought, he was raising his feet only to put them back down in almost exactly the same spot.

At last we came to the jetty where the large boats were docked. The bank sloped down at an alarming angle, and there were laborers carrying bags of goods aboard on a shaky gangplank. Leaving my bag with Tun Tun, I clutched young Enemy Conqueror's hand and inched down to the head of the gangplank. There was a man who looked as though he was in charge of the vessel, checking the goods. The boat, painted a crisp white, had the name Pyay Gyi D'kun, "Banner of the Mighty Country," emblazoned on her prow.

Several minutes later, having shouted myself hoarse about tickets, a cabin, a space, anywhere at all, and receiving not a word in reply, I gave up and we climbed up the bank again.

The laborers passing by me muttered with understandable irritation as I kept getting in their way. Wiry, with thin, hard muscles, they carried heavy bags on their shoulders with their necks bent and bare toes gripping the sandy soil. Their sunburned, shirtless torsos gleamed with sweat.

Back at the cart, we learned that Tun Tun had found more passengers, along with what looked as though it was a whole household's worth of furnishings. A couple was to be let off in town when we were on our way to the Inland Water Transport Board office to get a proper ticket for me. There I could not miss getting a ticket, at least not if the office would still be open after we delivered a houseful of furniture.

"Not to worry," Tun Tun said, as he tied one mattress to the side of the cart. "Plenty of time." The other side of the cart was already hanging with pots, pans, and a couple of large bags, with more bags on the roof. Another mattress was inside the cart, with a few framed photos tied with string reverently settled on top of it. I thought that with this load, Fragrant Emerald would probably lie down in the dirt and refuse to budge, but much to my surprise, after we had all squeezed in, he went off at a much faster trot. Soon the furniture and its owners were unloaded and we were on our way.

When we arrived at the Inland Water Transport Board, the ticket office was still open. All the cabins were full but I could have a space in the enclosed front room at the bow right under the bridge. The other alternative was the third-class deck below the cabins where I would have to sleep out in the open, next to the benches of the canteen and the stove. I could easily curl up on the wooden floors of the front room and use my bag as a pillow, I thought. I had slept in worse places.

Relieved at getting a space booked ("Pay the manager on board"), I asked Tun Tun to take me to a clean hotel. At that point, Fragrant Emerald refused to let me climb into the cart, moving away a few inches so that I could not put my foot up the step. When I finally managed to claw my way up he would not move an inch from the ticket office. Tun Tun had to sweet-talk him with many cluck-clucks of his tongue before we were on our way.

A horse cart which had been waiting at the office started up nicely, and the driver wielding his whip called out to Tun Tun, "Hey, let me have that horse of yours for just one morning and watch me make him behave. I'll teach him."

Tun Tun was furious.

"That bastard! He'll whip my poor boy and break his spirit, how dare he suggest such a thing? I'll teach *him*, I will."

I had noticed that he never used his whip.

He dropped me off at a hotel, promising to pick me up before dawn the next morning.

"I'm going home now," he said. "Both my sons are hungry."

The front desk of the hotel asked if I wanted a basement room as it was cheaper. I was horrified—to stay underground with no windows? I felt sick at the thought. The only other room available, he said, was a special room on the first floor. When I asked the rate he hesitated before saying two thousand kyat.

"Yes! Yes!" I said. "It's okay, I'll take it."

I went up to my room and tried to sleep.

My pillow was like a rock.

CHAPTER FIVE

On the Banner

Next morning I was waiting in front of the hotel before daybreak. A horse cart stopped, but it was not drawn by Fragrant Emerald.

"Tun Tun asked me to pick you up," the driver called to me as I turned away. "He said you'd be waiting."

In the darkness that wrapped Bhamo, the cart clip-clopped and turned into a road filled with moving shapes and flickering candles. It was a roadside market with vendors setting up stalls; candlelight

and subdued voices made the scene look like an eerie medieval dream. Both sides of the narrow street were already packed with goods and people as we inched our way forward, the grey mare carefully putting her hooves down to avoid stepping on cabbages.

At the jetty passengers were getting on board, and I was relieved to see two gangplanks placed side by side. A few shops lit with oil lamps sold piles of cakes, buns in plastic boxes and bags, stewed fruit, soft drinks, and bottled water. I went to one and chose a box of ma ywe, puffed rice melded with caramelized sugar into crunchy blocks. It seemed a better choice than the dry-looking cakes or the buns stuffed with jam or custard, both of which I absolutely loathe. I may be well-known as a glutton but when the choices are only jam buns (or hamburgers) I stay hungry.

A very young girl offered to carry my bag, and I was glad to keep one hand on her shoulder as we walked over the gangplank. Tidily and cleanly dressed in shabby clothes, she had circles of thanakha paste on her cheeks. Her hair was tied in a small fountain on top of her head and in it were tucked two jasmine flowers. She came aboard and helped me look for the manager, a harassed-looking little man with hair falling into his eyes and gold-rimmed spectacles falling down his nose. The girl still held my hand, as if I could not be trusted to keep from falling overboard.

The manager ticked off my name on a list and led me to the front room, where I would have a space about three feet by six feet. There were toilets and bathrooms at the other end of the row of cabins, all very clean. I tipped the girl generously but folded the notes into her hand so that she would not notice how much I gave until later.

The room was divided in two by a curtain that ran lengthwise; one side held the manager's cabin and some men's quarters, with our side for passengers. The floor was carpeted in red, or what was once red. By now it was dingy with dirt, with a sort of soggy feel to it.

I had no mat and no blanket. I sat down gingerly, cringing when I felt the carpet on my bare feet, since we had to take off our shoes at the door.

At the far end, an elderly man whom I had noticed the day before at the ticket office sat on a rush mat with a young companion. We smiled at each other and he said he was seeing off his son. After a while, a man came up to them and told the young man he could share a cabin. They got up to leave, the father carrying the mat rolled under his arm. As he walked out the door, I frantically called out to him to sell the mat to me, as his son would not need it anymore. He was reluctant, but after looking at the carpet he took pity on me. I was overjoyed—saved from sleeping in the soggy dirt! I laid out the mat and positioned my bag to serve as a pillow.

Our half of the room was filling up with what looked like one large family of Shan-Chinese. I found out from their chatter that they were members of an extended family, along with some neighbors who were in a sense relatives as well: "yut swe yut myo," or related by living in the same neighborhood. They laid out mats to cover all the carpeted area and were taking out thick woolen blankets. As they talked to each other about how cold it was going to be at night, a girl setting out her mat next to me suggested that I borrow a blanket from the manager since he usually had spare ones to lend to passengers.

I thanked her and found him among the milling crowd on the lower level. When I requested a blanket, he looked up from his papers and nodded without saying a word. He looked more harassed than before, poor man. I went back up to the salon, not expecting much, but in less than ten minutes the curtain behind my head was parted by an unseen hand and a thick new blanket was dumped on my lap. I looked up in surprise: it was the elderly, thick-set, and tall man I had noticed earlier, setting out cardboard boxes as garbage bins around the deck.

"Take that," he said gruffly. "It's brand new. I just bought it for a friend in Mandalay. You can use it during the trip."

The curtains were abruptly redrawn and he disappeared, but his voice stayed with me. It would be rude of him to criticize me to my face, but if he were unseen and just talking to himself, I could not take umbrage. Indeed I did not and I listened respectfully to his scolding.

"One should not travel too light," he reminded himself loudly. "It's so chilly on the river that people can get sick. Whenever one travels, at least a mat and blanket must be taken along, one never knows."

I found out later that he was the cleaner on the boat, sweeping up the litter of candy wrappers and other detritus, or washing the bathrooms and toilets several times a day, keeping them spanking clean and splashing wet. He would grunt with satisfaction when I emptied the plastic bag of trash I kept by my "bed" into his cans. In spite of his lowly status, he was treated with deference by the whole crew, for not only was he elderly—and old age enjoys respect at all levels in Myanmar—he had the dignity and confidence of a man who knows that the true value of a man does not dwell in his wealth or rank.

As he reprimanded me, the girl who had her space next to mine raised her eyebrows and smiled, and we giggled silently. She took out a small cassette player and started listening to songs that fortunately I liked as well, while her family put away tiffin carriers of food and snacks in bulging baskets.

A fat, very pretty baby girl crawled all over the mats. When she found a small hole in one of them, she plunked herself down and with serious concentration kept poking her little finger in it. Outside a woman leaned over the railings and shouted instructions to her husband about looking after their baby: "Don't feed him sweets, he'll get a cough, and don't let him go near the stove or play in the dust! Be sure to change his nappy when you get back home!"

The husband roared back, "I *know! I know!* And I already changed his *nappy this morning!*"

A young woman, obviously and alarmingly very pregnant, took up the space below my feet, separated by eighteen inches of space. Her space had actually been booked by a wiry, elderly sergeant major but because she was the wife of someone in his platoon, he had given her his place. He and her husband would sleep on the lower deck.

All the passengers in our side of the salon were women, but that was not by regulation. If a man had a ticket for this area he would be allowed to sleep in his corner, although the boat management tried to make sure that strangers were separated by gender and the man himself would if possible find a space elsewhere.

There were only two other women, apart from the pregnant girl and me, who were not in the Shan family party. The members of this group, about twenty strong, occupied most of the cabins as well. It was difficult to keep count, as they would stroll in and out, nap, eat, or just sit around chatting. The baby, named Thinn Thiri Khaing, or "Fragrant Noble Strong," was still diligently digging her way to the other side of the world through her hole in the mat. Everybody fussed over her, kissed, and cuddled her—all of which she bore patiently before going back to work with her little finger.

The presence of Fragrant Noble Strong ensured that the talk would turn to babies. One matronly lady complained that her neighbor was so jealous of anyone loving her granddaughter that she would not allow the baby to be taken over to the neighbors' houses to be bathed and cared for.

"She won't allow us to look after the child," she complained, "when we offer to take her for the afternoon and give her baths and feed her. She said the child might not love her family so much if strangers take care of her. Really, blood will tell, of course she will love her family more, but as neighbors we have a right to love her too. That woman's so selfish not to share the baby with us. Children are always a treasure, but you know. If you are wealthy, you seldom have children, and if you are poor you have many. It is life's way of balancing your happiness. You have one or the other, wealth or children, never both."

"True, true," the others muttered.

"It's better not to be too rich, either," she concluded with satisfaction. "Enough is good enough."

"True, true," the others muttered again and one young man added, "You're right; too much wealth gives you worries."

This last statement is something I have heard from all levels of society in my country. We even have a saying that people can suffer the pain of poverty but not the pain of wealth. If a bag of diamonds drops onto their laps, that's great, they won't refuse it, but if nothing like that happens, they say they are lucky they do not have to worry about losing it. Enough money to be comfortable and secure is the proper amount, everyone says, and they seem sincere when they say it.

Suddenly I heard a long toot that announced we were off, and I went out to the deck to watch the shore as it receded into the thinning mist, now streaked with rays of yellow sunlight.

Then I went exploring below deck. Three long tables and benches were set around a small space next to a fridge whose door was tied up with a chain and lock. Behind it was a small window leading to the kitchen. I decided it was better not to peer too closely into its sanitary conditions.

Most of the third-class passengers were carrying goods in baskets and some were actually setting up shops. These were up-turned crates offering a selection of sweets and cigarettes, some cheroots, and the makings of betel: leaves, nuts cut in slivers, lime paste, shreds of tobacco, cloves, and sugared coconut strands that had been colored red. Next to these were some wizened apples and wrinkled oranges displayed on a "counter" of the shop that also sold la hpet, or pickled tea leaf salad, a favorite and even honored snack of Myanmar. Ceremonies are never without these tea leaves that have been plucked, steamed, and buried for six months. Eaten with nuts and deep-fried beans, la hpet tastes like strong pesto.

Glory be, right next to the la hpet stall was the lending library! These "libraries" are highly popular and can be found in almost every convenience store on every city street corner, in villages, and on trains and boats. The younger generation loves to read, from the silliest cheap romance to great literature, poetry, essays, and translated works, which range from *War and Peace* to *Who Moved*

My Cheese? to the *Chicken Soup* series.

However, the choice of reading material on board was not that interesting. There were piles of comics, magazines about movie stars, and some novels. Predictably, the novels were about rich-boy-meets-poor-girl or vice versa, with all ending well.

At least there was something to read. I had forgotten to bring a book on this trip as I had thrown them out of my baggage on Christmas Day when I thought I was not going on this journey after all. I chose a few of the newer books as they smelled less foul, because after passing through many hands, literature printed on pulpy paper tends to pick up a distinct aroma.

Carrying my find back into the salon, I nearly tripped over the legs of the enormous pregnant girl. I apologized in terror, afraid that I might have done something to dislodge her baby. She sat up, smiled, and asked if she might borrow a magazine, so I let her choose one.

She may have sensed my apprehension—and everyone else's—about the possibility of dealing with a birth midstream. Probably wishing to reassure me and others that we would not be too inconvenienced if the baby arrived as we traveled, she told me she worked as a midwife in the military camp at Bhamo. Collective sighs of relief came from her audience as soon as we heard the words, "I'm a midwife."

Birth is a subject dear to the hearts of our women, and while before this young mother-to-be had been ignored in consideration of her shyness, now everybody clustered around her. She discussed her profession animatedly with us, the magazine forgotten, and I learned just about everything a person needs to know about pregnancy, childbirth, and looking after babies. When she admitted she was also worried her baby might arrive unexpectedly, we all to a woman said, "Not to worry! Just don't pass out on us, tell us what to do."

I sat reading the novels, hating every word of the cliché-ridden declarations of undying love but needing to read something, anything. When the love stories got to be too much for me, I would lie down with my eyes closed and my ears pricked to catch the ebb and flow of conversation around me.

I had found out earlier at what time we would be passing through the Second Defile. At that hour, I was on the upper deck by the bridge, waiting for a turn in the river after which would appear a majestic cliff.

On the top deck, a thin, middle-aged man leaned against the railings on the prow, from time to time calling instructions to a plump man on the bridge who clutched the wheel with a grim look on his face. I asked the thin gentleman if he could warn me when the cliff was about to come into sight.

When I told him that I had come through the First Defile, for an instant his expression "splintered," as we say in our language, myet hna pyet, becoming upset. After a brief silence, his face regained its composure and he said very gently and slowly, "Please, don't do that again, ever, that is a dangerous route."

As we stood in the icy breeze and golden sunlight, the cliff came into view on the right bank, and on an outcrop of rock halfway up sparkled a whitewashed stupa.

A few minutes later, we passed the Parrot's Beak, a rock protruding from the cliff in the shape of a parrot's head. The head had been painted green with round, white-rimmed eyes and the beak a brilliant, beautiful red. The head was slanted a bit as if the parrot were looking up at us; it seemed very lifelike. The river was narrow at this point and our boat gave a long toot that echoed and bounded off the cliffs along the banks.

The captain said that once upon a time a waterfall had cascaded down the cliff; when he was young, the jungles had been so thick that he had seen animals coming down to drink at the river at sunset. He added that when the water level reached the tip of the parrot's beak, boat travel through the Second Defile was dangerous. If the water rose higher or dropped lower, it was all right. As we passed, the parrot eyeing us critically, I was glad that the water level was low.

When we reached Shwegu the passengers rushed ashore to get food, and I bought a large grilled fish, intending it for a late-night snack.

New passengers struggled to get their luggage aboard. In the mêlée, I noticed an odd-looking man dressed all in brown in the style of a hermit, but instead of wearing a hermit's tall brown hat, his thick white hair was coiled in a neat knot on top of his head. He looked as though he was in his late seventies, with keen, intelligent eyes; his long, grey beard fell almost to his chest. He stalked aboard holding a thick wooden staff topped with the head of a carved naga or magical dragonlike serpent, its body twined along the length of the pole. The carving was not finely done but its rough execution gave it a raw power that made the staff look menacing. Interesting, I thought, and vowed to myself I would find out more about him before we reached Mandalay.

That would be easy, as he seemed to know the Shan women in my salon quite well and they greeted each other in a friendly but decidedly unreligious manner. Later he joined in their card games, and I noticed that he noticed that I was watching from the corner of my eye. He didn't play very well.

I was ready for lunch well before noon and I thought I should not delay going to the canteen. Some people were already eating rice and curry, and after peering at their plates I decided to have pork. The rice was coarse, the soup thin and watery, and the pork curry was tough, oily, and tasteless. Unable to eat any of this, I ordered one fried egg, sunny side up. Told that one serving was three eggs, nothing less, I thought briefly of my sky-high cholesterol level but what the heck, the pork was revolting.

As we went past Shwegu, I remembered that it was somewhere around here that the fishermen were helped by Ayeyarwaddy dolphins. Ancient Chinese texts noted that in this river there lived "sea pigs." Dolphins must have looked piglike to them as they are rotund, without scales, and of a blackish color. A friend had suggested to me once that the flesh of the dolphin would look like pork, since both have the same three layers of rind, fat, and flesh, but I hoped against hope that dolphins were never eaten by anybody anywhere.

The Ayeyarwaddy fishermen do not eat the dolphins, that's for sure, since they are considered "kyayzu shin," someone you owe a debt to. Dolphins help them catch fish. The men rap on the sides of their boats with a wooden stick in a certain tempo, and the dolphins come up to see what's what. If they know the men, and most are regular helpers, they circle around schools of fish to drive them into the nets and flip their fins to tell when the nets should be pulled in. The men recognize the dolphins by their color, shape, or size and have given them names, much as though they were pet dogs.

Our boat stopped at Katha, where the Shweli River comes down from the far mountains of China, flows into the Ayeyarwaddy River, and adds to its speed. Forests of teak and other hardwood trees line the banks here, along with abundant wild game. Sir Harcourt Butler, Deputy Governor of "Burma" during the colonial period, liked to arrange shooting parties for his friends during the Christmas holidays; it is said that salt licks were set up all year round in the vicinity to ensure ample game come December, and that the air stank of blood for weeks after the Christmas hunting holiday. The Buddhists of the region could never understand how anyone could celebrate his Savior's birth by killing other creatures, when they themselves set free birds, fish, and even bigger game on Buddhist holy days.

Smelling the grilled fish next to my pillow on a plastic bag, I began to feel hungry even though I'd had that heavy lunch, but thought I should not give in too easily to my greed. I fell into a deep and drugged-like sleep, waking up with a start when the tempo of the engines changed. Our boat was stuck fast on a hidden sandbank.

The Shan group dozed while recently boarded Kachin ladies sat up discussing the dangers of boat travel. One of them prayed aloud, swearing an oath which one normally hears only in classical plays, that she was a good Buddhist. If celestial beings found this to be true, she begged, would they please protect us from a watery grave? Stuck as we were, I felt that what we needed now was to get into deeper water, but maybe she knew more than I did about the tantrums of the river.

I heard one young widow discussing her upcoming marriage. She said she was marrying her childhood sweetheart, who was now a widower. It seemed like happy fate, but she worried about the children both would bring to this union, three of hers and two of his. Her companions all gave different and contradictory advice.

In our culture we have not gone past the fairy-tale attitudes of cruel stepmothers or stepfathers, and I felt this couple would have a difficult time because of outsiders meddling, taking sides, and urging conflict. Neighbors and relatives give a lot of warmth and care but even with all good intentions, they can interfere enough in a marriage to destroy it. This marriage sounded doomed to me unless the couple moved away from all the people they knew.

The boat was waiting for another to come by and pull it out, but for some hours river traffic had only been small sampans or tiny motorboats that weren't powerful enough to rescue us. A zay thinbaw, or "market boat," passed by but it was too heavily laden to drag us off the shoals.

Patience is the noblest virtue of my people ("Patience," we say, "can even bring Buddhahood"), and the women in my room sat patiently eating pickled plums, pickled tea leaves, and sunflower seeds. Again they were talking about babies and birth with the pregnant midwife. One of them fed Fragrant Noble Strong some pickled tea leaves, saying she had better learn to eat everything while still young or else she would be a picky eater later. The baby chewed with enthusiasm.

I headed for the canteen with a plastic bowl to bring back water so I could wash my hands before dining on my grilled fish later that night. As I stalked grumpily toward the stairs, bored with being marooned, I glanced up and nearly dropped my bowl.

The flat riverbank was just above my eye level so all I could see were a few clumps of scraggly grass. Then, from behind them, looking as if it were only a few feet away, rose the full moon, fat and pale yellow, and so incredibly huge that at first I did not know what it was.

Startled out of my wits, I gave a most inelegant shriek and then stood watching it with my mouth open. It rose in slow majesty until it half disappeared behind some grey clouds that looked as flimsy as thin silk. People going to and from the baths bumped into me but I stood rooted to my spot, gaping like a village idiot. I heaved a deep sigh of complete satisfaction when it finally disappeared from view behind a thick cloud.

I did not have the chance to eat my grilled fish that night, although it had been on my mind all day, for promptly at 9 p.m. the lights went out. As we all snuggled down, I heard a few giggles and thought about how much this was like nights in a girls' dormitory in a convent school, if only I disregarded the presence of pregnant women or widows about to remarry.

CHAPTER SIX

The New Year... or Not

It was a very cold night but thanks to my borrowed blanket, I was comfortable. I woke up before dawn when the engines revved. We were off!

The Kachin ladies would soon leave us at Katha, and in the icy dawn they took baths and smeared freshly ground thanakha all over, including their legs and arms. The fragrance filled our salon, a heady perfume. I snuggled in the cold, longing to have my warm cat Marmalade snoring in my arms.

By daybreak we were stuck again.

I went up to the top deck, looking around at the slightly misty morning. On my left the reddish glow of the sky over the distant tree line turned brighter as the sun came up, blushing pink and looking as fragile as a pretty thirteen-year-old girl. On my right, the moon was setting behind a low range of dark hills, its pale, translucent face soft against the purple sky. A moonset and a sunrise at the same time! I felt blessed as my head swiveled like a spectator's at a tennis match to catch the sun-moon magic.

A boat came by at last with an engine powerful enough to tow us, and we were soon on our way, reaching Htee Jaint in the late afternoon. A wide expanse of sandbank fronted the village so that disembarking passengers faced a long hike, but there were bullock carts and trishaws waiting at the jetty for those unable to face the strenuous walk. A few young women with trays on their heads sold packed lunches: rice, curry, and a relish wrapped in leaves and tied with strips of bamboo. On the opposite bank, I glimpsed golden pagodas with their tips of jeweled crowns flashing in the blazing sunlight as we departed.

I had read all the novels in the lending library except the translated kung fu novels. As I sat on the deck by the railings trying to make sense of *The Clutching Claws of the Green Dragon* or *The Whip Wielded by Princess Jade Mountain*, three girls sat by me, applying polish to each other's toes from an array of bottles. One favored a peach tint, while the other two liked bright blue and deep mauve. Feeling this colorful scene to be too much in combination with kung fu masters ripping out intestines, I went to lie down in my narrow space with a groan of nausea.

A card game of great intensity and low stakes was going on, with the bearded "recluse" playing and—as usual—losing. The gamblers seemed determined to wait out all delays with their deck of cards, while I, who could barely play solitaire, had no hope of joining them.

When I saw the Bearded One stretch himself and say, "I've had it for the day," I casually got up from my place and went out on deck, hoping he would come for a breath of fresh air. I had been longing to know the story behind his dark clothes and his long beard.

He did come out to lean on the railings a few feet away. Probably he too was intrigued by a woman traveling alone and obviously not in a normal career. He had heard one of the passengers remark when I was writing one morning that I must be a doctor because my penmanship was so bad. I had said, "Unfortunately no," and did not elaborate.

Considering my age and his, I thought it would be all right if I began talking to him; I had to get his story. His long beard hinted at many possibilities, and once he began talking I was not disappointed.

"Once I was a captain in the infantry," he said, "back in the mid-1950s under U Nu's government. Then I went to join the BCP."

I was astounded. U Nu had presided over a fourteen-year

period of democracy, and the Burma Communist Party was an insurgent organization that had set off a civil war in Myanmar as soon as we gained independence. For a military man to join the BCP was a 180-degree turn; the military, even under the Socialist regime from 1962 to 1988, had fought the Communists for forty years all over the country.

He went on as if he knew my ears were pricked like a cat's.

"Then, about three years later I surrendered and came back 'into the fold,'" he said with a smile. "The army officers I had worked under were quite willing to have me return to the military and I went back for a year."

A returnee from a BCP camp would not be so easily accepted back into the ranks. Was he trying to tell me that he had been sent to infiltrate the BCP? I opened my mouth to ask but thought better of it.

"But I felt I did not belong," he continued, "and I left the army to spend my life in meditation. I went to a place in the mountains I once passed through when I was a BCP soldier."

There, he had met a few men who were meditating, and one had very briefly told him how and why they meditated in the Thama Hta method.

Its goal involves gaining magical powers such as the ability to embark upon astral travel, or to manufacture lodestones, or to gain the power of healing by the laying on of hands. Thama Hta is widely practiced all over Myanmar by young and old, laypeople as well as monks and nuns.

"Now I travel to places where I have to be at certain times to meditate," he said. He had just returned from the A Laung Daw Kathappa Wildlife Sanctuary, not to watch birds but to meditate near the holy shrine that is found there.

My ascetic companion said he lived part of the time in Thanlyin, a pretty town across a river from Yangon, and told me the name of his neighborhood.

"Ask any horse-cart driver for U Maung Maung," he told me, citing a name so common that it belonged to half the male population, "and they'll tell you where I live. Come visit me sometime and try meditating."

I do like my privacy, but to sit alone without my laptop or DVD player was not entirely my thing, so I said I would visit him, maybe, and smiled sweetly. Who knows what supernatural powers he had; I felt I should be ultragracious. Afterward, every time I saw him I would catch his eye and give a slight but reverent bow. I was afraid he would turn me into a frog if I looked disrespectful.

We arrived in Tagaung by evening, just as the sun's deep yellow rays struck the jetty. An old man was struggling to carry up water in two yoked pails, looking as if he had been dipped in molten gold, pails and all. My ascetic acquaintance went regally down the gangplank with his dragon-headed staff held high. When he disembarked, I felt sorry to see him go, but also relieved.

We spent the night at Tagaung and I woke up before midnight, remembering it was New Year's Eve. I imagined my friends partying hard as we do every year, but I couldn't stay awake to ring in the New Year and fell back to sleep in seconds. It was only months later that I realized I had privately observed the New Year one day early, on the thirtieth rather than the customary thirty-first of December.

But then, with my inherent confusion of not knowing my left hand from my right or whether it is Tuesday or Wednesday, my losing a day or two would surprise nobody who knows me. After all, one year I didn't notice the entire month of August until it had finally passed me by.

PART II

The Central Plains

CHAPTER SEVEN
Mandalay, Mon Amour

The shudder of revving engines woke me early and I snuggled deeper into my thick blanket for a snooze, with a delicious sense of well-being spreading inside me. This morning, maybe to celebrate being much nearer our destination or perhaps to help us avoid another submerged sandbank, a monk's sermon was played over the loudspeakers. Fortunately the speaker in our area was broken, so we could hear it only faintly without having it pierce our eardrums.

Myint Myint Htwe, our mother-in-waiting, looked cheerful.

"I'm getting nearer to Mother!" she announced to all of us. She admitted she too had been worried about the baby arriving while she was traveling, but I was not too sure any of us should be feeling relieved so soon. After all, we still had some miles to go and heaven forbid, maybe a few more sandbanks in our path.

Lunch, which I hoped would be the last meal I would enjoy at the canteen, was awful and I had my usual three fried eggs.

With no interest in my food, I talked to the boys serving me, who told me that they were brothers—five of them. They had three sisters living in Mandalay with their mother, who had single-handedly brought up the eight kids after their father disappeared when they were still very young.

"Where did he go? Didn't you try to find him?" I asked.

"Mother was too proud to go looking for him or to ask her in-laws," one of them answered, as casually as if I had inquired about a misplaced book. "You see, when they married, Father's family was far wealthier than Mother's and they did not approve of her. She thought he'd gone back to them."

After they had eight kids together? He might have drowned or met with an accident or wandered around in a fog of amnesia, but that proud woman refused to ask if anyone had seen him. I have met many Burmese women with this sort of pride, far too many of them in my own coterie of aunts, cousins, and nieces, but I took my hat off to this one.

By midmorning we were passing the immense, unfinished Mingun Pagoda rising like a square mountain out of the flat plains. The slopes of the riverbanks had been lined with concrete and here women had laid out their laundry in neat rows. Most of the clothes were longyi, those sarongs in tube shapes, and their colorful squares made the slopes look like a giant quilt.

I gave the blanket back to the old man who had lent it to me and knelt to "kadaw," or bow three times to him on my knees, holding out several thousand kyat "for his medicine" with both hands, which is the polite way to give money. He accepted this with proper dignity, after blessing me with good health, success, and safe travels.

After disembarking, I shared a horse cart with two monks. I sat up front by the driver so that I would not be sitting close to either of them, since it is not permissible for a woman to touch any part of a monk's robe, let alone his flesh.

Even with monks, I can't resist chatting. I learned one of them had entered the order at age thirteen, and now at twenty, he was no longer a novice but finally a monk. One must be twenty to be a monk, and he looked very proud to have obtained this status. His name, he told me, was U Waiza Nanda, a Pali name given to him when he entered the order, and he lived at Mya Taung Monastery.

Mya Taung! It was the monastery donated by King Thibaw's strong-minded queen Supaya Lat. I asked if any trace of the original monastery remained, as it had been destroyed in World War II.

"Only the stairs," the young monk said. "Nothing else remains."

The monastery I had seen in old photos had been exquisite.

After dropping off the monks, I went to buy a ticket to Yangon for the day after next, and from the airline office I took a taxi to the home of Chan Aye and Phyu Mon.

Chan Aye is a very talented painter and sculptor, and his wife is an equally talented writer and performance artist. They live with their teenage son, a nervous cat, and a very obese dog in a pretty brick cottage with a Japanese-style garden filled with Chan Aye's carvings.

Both Chan Aye, which means "Cool and Calm," and Phyu Mon, which means "White Purity," are dedicated artists who are just as dedicated to hospitality. They were happy to see me arrive as unexpectedly as if I had dropped from a tree and were only sorry I would be leaving the next day. That was the reason why I bought my ticket before setting foot in their house: they would have persuaded me to stay a week if I did not have it already in hand.

We had a quick lunch before we set off to visit our photographer friend, U Chit Wain.

U Chit Wain is the only son of wealthy parents, and is married but childless. At seventy-eight he lives with his wife and mother; Mum is still very much alive and alert at near one hundred. Pampered from birth but not at all spoiled, U Chit Wain's obsession is photography, and he has diligently practiced this for most of his life. He has a bicycle that he rides out to the suburbs or villages near Mandalay, with his gear in the carrier basket and usually with someone to accompany him, since his mother still worries about her "baby boy" and will not allow him to drive a car ("Such a dangerous thing!"). If he wants to go out, he has to go with someone that she trusts to look after him. As his peers are no longer as healthy as he is, and in some cases not even alive, his chaperones get younger with each decade.

He is a true gentleman with a great sense of humor and he

does not lack companions, especially in a town like Mandalay where the intelligentsia enjoy a great reverence from the younger people. U Chit Wain once knew the "greats" of Mandalay intimately: composers, writers, poets, singers, artists, dancers, and sculptors who have all passed away by now.

We went out for coffee and sat talking about his work. He was smoking furiously now that he was out of the house, as he still dared not smoke in front of Mother. Only recently had he ever exhibited his photos, and he gave me one of a boy racing through the shallows of the Ayeyarwaddy: the sand and waves and boy coated with the gold of the setting sun, and splashes of water glinting like scattered gold bullion.

The next morning I went to the Maha Gandayone Monastery to deliver some books to a cousin, who was studying there as a monk. He was away so I left the books in the office—just in time to witness the monks and novices arrive in silent rows at the dining hall, where the donor for that day was serving lunch.

Rice was being scooped up from three gigantic pots, and pork stew simmered in a wok that looked like an upturned six-foot satellite dish. The cook stirring this with a spoon the size of an oar smiled when she saw me sniffing at the stew and said that after the monks had eaten I could join the laypeople for lunch if I wanted. (When good food is under my nose I often look hungry, and many people throughout my life, everywhere, have offered to feed me because of this.)

The lines of monks walked on bare feet, stepping slowly. The older monks were at the front; the lines were arranged, it seemed, by age. As they passed with eyes lowered, I sat on a curb by the path with my feet tucked behind me. My eyes were respectfully lowered so I saw only their feet. In my country where the hot weather makes us prefer open slippers, I am a great believer that the cleanliness of feet marks the personality of the person. All the feet I saw that day were scrubbed clean, with well-trimmed toenails. Just out of curiosity, I sat there inspecting toes until the whole procession had passed.

Boys dressed in white made up the rear. They were not novices but Po Thudaw, sort of valets to the monks. They enter the monastery in that role first to learn discipline. They run errands, sweep the compound, and perform other menial tasks before being ordained as novices and then, after reaching twenty years of age, they become monks. All the novices and monks in this monastery had first started as Po Thudaw, unlike in other monasteries, for the Maha Gandayone is a very strict monastic college for scholar monks.

Without staying for lunch, I walked over to the mile-long wooden U Bein Bridge spanning Taungthaman Lake, very near the monastery. As I crossed over to the other side, little girls stood here and there along the bridge. Hoping to have their photos taken by tourists from whom they could demand pocket money in return, they had adorned themselves with bunches of flowers that covered their heads, thick thanakha paste applied like concrete, lips red as if coated with blood, and eyes thickly rimmed in black kohl. They looked like strange mutants, and some tourists I saw did take a few photos. What their friends back home would make of these fiendish-looking girls, I could not imagine, but I hoped they would not think this was the usual getup for local children.

After lunch back at Chan Aye and Phyu Mon's house, I took a long nap before we went out to dinner at the best Chinese restaurant in Mandalay. I was sleepy still, but my spirits revived with the great food and an electrically motivated fish on a plaque that sang "Merry Christmas" as it flapped its tail. I had seen this advertised in foreign magazines as the silliest gift for Christmas and I agreed heartily. It was silly and kept us giggling into our food.

When we got home, I persuaded shy Phyu Mon to show me the performance art piece she would present during a tour of Japan the following month.

She darkened a large room and lit a few candles in the corners. There was a bare-branched tree in a pot looking stark and sad, with eggshells hanging from it that turned into translucent marble in the candlelight. Soft, almost imperceptible music played and Phyu Mon's fingers twirled in graceful movements as they hovered around the shells. Her hands looked like wings of a dying white dove as I watched, enchanted.

CHAPTER EIGHT

The Height of Luxury: On the Road to Mandalay

It's common knowledge now, over a century after Rudyard Kipling wrote his poem, that on the actual route to Mandalay up the Ayeyarwaddy River there are no flyin' fishes that play, nor dawn that comes up like thunder outer China 'crost the Bay. We shall forgive him, as he was merely exercising his right to poetic license even if he stretched its limits—and our geographical boundaries—to near collapse.

A year after my vagabond voyage from Bhamo to Mandalay when I had slept under a borrowed blanket with a pregnant woman at my feet, I was now literally on the Road to Mandalay, traveling on a luxury tourist cruise ship of that same name. This floating five-star hotel runs between Mandalay and Bagan and I have been on it several times as guest lecturer, giving talks on culture.

I was met at the airport in Mandalay by a taxi sent by the ship, and I found the driver typical of the up-country people ... witty, proud of his country, and full of goodwill or cedana, which is an integral part of our culture. Ko Hla Moe was not embarrassed to tell me that before he drove foreigners around, he had no idea that they would enjoy seeing the villages. He had always thought our pagodas would be the main draw, but I told him that tourists get "pagoda-ed out" after coming upon one behind almost every bend in the road.

Our road wended its way past small villages of bamboo houses. I noticed that the bamboo matting of the walls was finely, densely woven. The houses were built on stilts with three sides walled in on the ground floor level. A veranda ran around the front of the upper floor, which had folding doors all along its length so that the whole upper area could be open to the elements during the day, or on warm nights. Typical up-country Burmese houses have only one walled-in corner on the upper floor to be used as a dressing room and to store trunks of clothing, plus folded bedding during the day.

The wooden floors are kept shining with frequent applications of wax; at night the family places their bedding on those gleaming surfaces and folds pads and pillows away at dawn when they get up.

The side and back walls of the upper floor have windows with a door hinged on the top, propped up with a stick. Spacious, uncluttered and cool—I longed to have a house like that in Yangon.

"I take tourists to the villages and people invite them in for green tea," Ko Hla Moe said to me as my mind wandered through the houses. "They may only have a few pieces of palm sugar or a saucer of sugar to offer with it, but they still offer it, and somehow with sign language they all sit there chatting and smiling. I like seeing that, locals and foreigners connecting without words."

I could well believe what Ko Hla Moe said of the villagers offering whatever edibles they may have on hand. In my wanderings, children have offered me bananas, and adults have presented a share of their lunch box or tea, peanuts, plums and other fruits of the orchard—all from complete strangers I had met barely a minute before.

Once I walked into a Palaung village in the far north and, after happily greeting me like her long-lost daughter, one old lady scampered into her kitchen. When I followed and asked her to come out for a chat, she said she was cooking dinner for me. As it was nearly dark and I faced a two-hour drive on dark roads back to town, it took all the time I had left to beg her not to cook anything because I could not stay.

A stranger looking at us would have thought I was a daughter about to abandon Mum (although my own mother in Yangon, if I had dropped by at her house, would barely have waggled her fingers at me if she were deep in a book). We Myanmar people are a friendly lot but especially so in the countryside, and I'm grateful that most of our population still lives in rural areas.

Ko Hla Moe and I soon arrived at the Inwa jetty, where the river was wide and deserted. There were no small steamers, paddle boats, or bamboo rafts to be seen, as the current was too strong. The waters were flowing at a run, the waves helter-skelter chasing each other downstream.

I walked up the Road to Mandalay's wide gangplank where Esther, the new manager, was waiting to welcome me aboard. Although German, this lovely young woman always wore Burmese clothing when she was on duty and often when she was off. She had not been long in Myanmar but already behaved like a perfect Burmese lady. Her gentle demeanor and decorous behavior was exactly that of a well-bred girl raised from birth in Mandalay.

(It has always frustrated me that I could never achieve that demeanor if I lived to be two hundred. My impatience and sarcastic tongue leave no room for decorum and, knowing my limitations, I have abandoned hope. Mum told me that she gave up on me when I was seven, after I tried to strangle our dentist. He was wearing a tie while trying to pull my baby teeth, and for a dentist to wear a tie when treating children is risky business indeed. I nearly succeeded and the top anesthetist of the day had to be summoned to put my lights out while six other dentists held me down.)

At dinner that evening the table next to mine had a lively discussion on what they had seen and done in Mandalay with their different tour guides. One couple described their lunch at a local eatery, which sounded as though they had been served grilled milk curds in a curry. For this dish, thick curds are first squeezed of all liquid, wrapped in lotus leaves, and then lightly grilled. The dense, round cakes are then cubed and deep-fried or cooked in a curry, or as a salty, spicy relish with tomatoes. This is typical Mandalay fare and I was glad they liked it, for the strong flavors of our food can at times overwhelm delicate foreign taste buds.

One group had been taken to a large tea shop, where they saw gem traders sitting on tiny kindergarten-sized chairs around low tables and brokering deals. When business was slow they played pool at a table in the shed next door.

I overheard one traveler asking the others if they knew what happened to the "holes" cut from pieces of jade when bracelets are made. I pricked up my ears; I didn't know either. He described how he saw these circles of thick jade being carved by women into delicate pendants. Beautifully intricate things, he said. Just when I was thinking I must get myself some, he added that he could not buy any of them; they were all to be sold wholesale and probably would be exported to China.

A couple from the next table was fascinated by a water clock they had seen used as a timer at a place where people hammer gold into gold leaf. Another told us how his wife had admired a small item priced at one thousand kyat (less than a dollar) but decided not to buy it, only to have the shopkeeper give it to her as a gift.

"What generosity," the wife chipped in. "I haven't encountered anything like that in any other place."

After dinner there was a classical dance performance in the lounge. The guests had spent a rough day sightseeing in Mandalay, where the September weather was humid and damp. Most of them in their seventies and older, they chose to linger in the dining room with bottles of good wine. So for the first part of the show, the only audience was Esther, her assistant, a guide, and me. We clapped madly, and both performers and audience were relieved when some of the diners finally joined us.

The night sky was clear, stars shimmering like jewels. Before going to bed, I stood at the railing and looked across at the flickering lights of Sagaing, my father's hometown which he left for good when he went off to the university in Yangon.

I tried to imagine my sophisticated father when he was a boy growing up in this highly conservative town. My grandfather was the only legitimate son of a wealthy landowner who had about twenty mistresses—all living in his house and spending most of his money. Grandfather chose not to remain at home to manage the fast-dwindling family fortune but instead studied law at Calcutta University, after which he rose to be a judge under the colonial British. My father was sent off to Saint Peter's, a boarding school in Mandalay, while his parents were posted all over the country, taking his much younger siblings with them. I could imagine him as an aloof, lonely little boy with his head in a book at all times.

Although educated in the Western way, my grandfather, or rather his conventional wife, still believed in old traditions. Father was their oldest son, born on a Saturday morning, and since first-born Saturday sons are considered bad luck, he was "sold" to his maternal aunt and her husband for twenty-five pya—a quarter of one kyat.

Father, who had not a conventional bone in his body, was irate his whole life that he was sold for such a measly amount, symbolic or not. This resentment gave him a cynical view of life, sharpened by his scathing wit.

My cousin from Mother's side, Nyo Gyi or "Big Brown," who was the boat's chief engineer, came up to my cabin to catch up on family news. I asked him when the crew would be having monhinga for breakfast. This fish broth is fragrant with lemongrass and pepper, and Myanmar people can hardly go a week without it—I know I can't. He said they usually have other more filling breakfasts but that he would ask the galley to cook it one day. Henceforth every morning I would ask the housekeeping staff, "Did you have monhinga for breakfast?" but the answer was always no. I began to get withdrawal pains.

At the last buffet lunch served on board before the end of our voyage, I ate my way through a few salads. Then, to balance the ungodly healthiness, I went to fetch a plateful of éclairs and a coconut cream dessert. The stately head chef Yannis passed my table and we smiled at each other, he no doubt remarking to himself that the éclair tray would need to be refilled at once. Just as I was spooning up the last of the coconut cream, I heard a lady standing at the buffet table ask a waiter what the soup of the day was. His answer was, "It's monhinga, madam, our traditional fish broth."

I stiffened in horror. I longed to jump up and get a bowl of it, but Yannis was still standing by the table greeting other guests. He had seen me eating *dessert*, so I could not go back now to get soup, for God's sakes! I sat in despair, debating with myself if I should risk looking ridiculous but even though I did not mind that, I realized I might bring disgrace to my country by eating soup after dessert. So I got no monhinga that day, and since then have been making up for the deficiency with bowls of it from a stall a block away from my flat.

During the cruise I got to know the guests and at times we talked politics in private. Visitors often see things in Myanmar that are totally at odds with what they have read in the international media and they want to understand what's going on. Without an in-depth study of our recent political history of say, the past thirty years, few could understand that an incident of today has its root cause in a singular and even unimportant action from decades past.

I think first-time visitors expect to find—although they are too polite to say so—Myanmar residents who cower in fear and despair, many of them poor and seeking handouts. When meeting people who no doubt have difficult lives, travelers find they are humorous, warm, proud, and dignified, spending what little they have on religious institutions. It is a conundrum, which some inhabitants of wealthy nations can't understand. Perhaps visitors don't see that we in Myanmar have an inner core of strength, which doesn't veer toward aggression but is rooted in the equanimity with which they face reality. We neither give in nor give up: we have the ability, acquired through our religious beliefs, to refuse to let life get us down. Tough lot, us.

One elderly tourist asked me, in all sincerity and bewilderment, how, since the people he saw were obviously poor, could they look so happy? I tried to explain, but I doubt if he understood, the concept that anybody could be happy with such a huge lack of wealth.

I have often heard from the guests of the Road to Mandalay how enchanted they were with Myanmar: "We have been to over one hundred countries but we have never seen such a lovely country as yours or met such wonderful people anywhere else." They especially liked the children in out-of-the-way villages.

I remember one young American woman asking me if we taught Spanish in our schools, for in one village a little girl had skipped up to her to greet her in Spanish. I nearly choked and said no, we hardly have enough English teachers, although English is taught as a second language in all schools from kindergarten on up; and that the girl probably learned Spanish from another tourist. After we stopped at the next village, the woman came back to tell me excitedly that she had taught a few French phrases to a group of children, and that they had repeated every word perfectly.

One morning as the ship neared Bagan, I gave my talk on spirits, or Nat, of which there are two kinds. One Nat exists in our Buddhist lore as celestial beings, much like Christian angels. The other Nat are the thirty-seven lords and ladies found in spirit worship: people who died violent deaths and cannot pass into the next life cycle, attached as they are through bitterness to their past. These Nat remain in limbo, like ghosts. The two groups share the same name, which at times has confused many a foreign scholar.

The most interesting of the thirty-seven lords and ladies must be the patron spirit of gamblers and drunks, jolly old Ko Gyi Kyaw. I told the audience how I took a bottle of cheap whiskey—six hundred kyat or sixty U.S. cents a bottle, and not tasting of turpentine either—to a spirit ceremony where everyone was welcome. We all watched the medium, called Nat Kadaw or Honored Wife of the Spirit, chug down my whiskey in several swallows, without showing the slightest effect from the alcohol. I was told later that it was the spirit who drank it, not him ... Yes, him, for most of these "wives" are transsexuals, who are teased but never violently harassed or treated with hatred.

These sassy mediums say they are born to the profession, for they can dress up, dance, have fun, and be as campy as they want, applying makeup as skillfully as the best gay artistes working in expensive beauty salons. A few have given me great makeup tips, taking pity on me for my own slapdash efforts.

Spirit ceremonies are all about making the gods happy with dance, music, drink, and food, and it's party, party, parteey with no evil, dark, or solemn practices. The music from the traditional orchestra with its mad thumps on drums, wails from oboes, and thundering clashes of cymbals can make your feet dance or your eardrums burst.

The more dignified Nat do not drink or dance too wildly when they possess their mediums and are regarded with great respect, but the bad-boy Nat are far more popular, I have found.

After I finished my talk and answered many questions, I was free and began to look forward to seeing Bagan. No matter how many times I go there, I am immediately wrapped in a sense of tranquility I find nowhere else. And this time I was on a quest, one that a hectic schedule had kept me from making for two years. It concerned the name of my country.

Myanmar has always been our country's name in our language, but the British called it Burma and thus it was known to the international world. Although we gained independence in 1948, neither the democratic government of U Nu nor the Socialist regime of U Ne Win changed the colonial name. When the military State Law and Order Restoration Council took power in 1989, it changed the name to the Union of Myanmar, doing away with the defunct and unwieldy Socialist Republic of the Union of Burma at the same time.

Because the military changed it, the name of Myanmar was unacceptable to many people, mostly those of Western countries, who insist on continuing to use Burma.

My view is, the military government did not get the name out of a hat and that actually it was the British who did so when they used "Burma." They probably confused it with the name of the majority race Bama (Burmese). I have even met a Brit who sniffed that "Myanmar" is a newly coined word which was obviously also new to us, the people of the country. I took two minutes of her time to explain that we had used this name for centuries, and since any farmer in my country who didn't speak English would hardly know what Burma was, let alone that it was the name of his country, I thought it was reasonable that it had been changed back to its original name of Myanmar.

I knew from our history books that there is a stone inscription from 597 ME (datable as 1235 CE) that provided the earliest mention of Myanmar Pyay, which literally means "Myanmar Country." I had no idea where this stone was until a couple of years ago, when a young computer geek gave me some photos with relevant data. The inscribed stone is in the Museum of Bagan, where it is one of many other inscriptions and is identified as Number 43. I wanted to see this for myself, and get a rubbing if possible.

My cousin Nyo Gyi headed for the airport one morning and dropped me off in front of the Museum of Bagan.

I knew the inscribed stones were in a large hall and I thought

I would simply stroll down the rows of inscriptions until I came to number 43. I should have remembered that every single time I have thought something would be a piece of cake, it has gone the opposite way with a vengeance. Dozens of stone inscriptions were there but the numbers jumped from the 50s to the 160s and back to the 30s which segued into the 90s. In no time I was scurrying all over the vast hall in total panic, taking deep breaths as I ran.

A young woman peeped into the hall at the sound of my footsteps echoing in the empty chamber and came over to ask if she could help. I could only gasp out what I was looking for ... "Number 43, it's number 43, I can't find it anywhere" ... and she helped me look for another fifteen minutes.

Noticing that I was getting increasingly wild-eyed, she gently suggested that I go see the assistant director. I have a horror of officialdom and at first refused, shaking my head vehemently. She assured me in a soothing voice that he was a very nice, helpful person. Reluctantly I allowed myself to be led away down some stairs and into an airy office where a man sat at his desk, shirt opened over an undershirt to ease the mounting heat of the day.

She said to him from the doorway, "A guest to see you, Saya," and left. Saya, literally meaning "teacher," is a polite and unofficial term of address for a man, which is useful if you don't know his name. So I called him that too, as I hurried over to him, my panic of the Lost Stone overcoming my panic of Facing Officialdom. Leaning over his desk I wailed my woes. He too had a look of alarm in his eyes at that point and jumped out of his chair, buttoning his shirt and saying yes, yes, he would definitely help me in any way he could.

"What's the name of the inscription?" he asked, after I explained to him how much I wanted to find this ancient stone.

It turned out that scholars and curators catalog the inscriptions by their names, and not by numbers. By now, my brain was completely devoid of any sensible thought, and I forgot that I had been carrying the data in my wallet ever since I was first told of the stone two years ago. I could only mumble that it was numbered 43, and that it was dated 597 ME, which makes it 1235 CE, and that it had the all-important words "Myanmar Pyay" on it.

He brought out a book of handwritten copies of stone inscriptions and I immediately recognized the handwriting as the one in my photo. Grabbing the book from him, I began to look through it page by page, while he searched in his bookcase for more information. I was still standing at his desk as I looked; he gently told me that I could sit down in his chair if I wanted, which I declined with a mumbled thank-you.

(As I look back on this, I realize that my behavior while asking help from a stranger had been most impolite, undignified and un-Myanmarlike. All awareness that dignity, patience, and decorum are the hallmark of good social behavior had fled my mind. Yeah well, they never dwell there so much at other times, I must admit.)

"Found it!" I yelped with joy.

"Good!" he replied. By now he was acting as if we were old friends, since I had vaulted over several stages of developing friendship within minutes.

He came over and looked at the page.

"I see, it's the Yadana Kon Htan inscription," he said. "That's not in the museum."

I thought I would faint dead away at his feet.

"It's in a storage facility," he added hastily, as I felt my face turn white. "I'll get someone to take you there. You also wanted a rubbing, right?"

I finally sat down, unsure that I would ever find the inscription, trying to breathe evenly and feeling very shaky. He began to make calls and soon said he had sent for somebody.

In ten minutes a slender, dark man in thick glasses arrived and was introduced as U Ko Ko, who knew how to make rubbings. We would go together to look for the stone. He would make a rubbing and have it delivered to the ship by evening.

I said goodbye with heartfelt thanks to the assistant director, who said he would call ahead to the official in charge to allow us to see the stone. U Ko Ko and I left, with him pushing his bicycle as we walked out the gates, planning to get a horse cart for me. It began to rain softly although it was still bright and sunny.

A man on a scooter whizzed by us and U Ko Ko gave a piercing whistle. Taxi service, I wondered, but no, it was his friend who would take me to our destination while U Ko Ko followed on his bike. I jumped on the seat, wishing it were a roaring Harley but happy to be able to get to "my" stone quickly. Suddenly it began to rain much harder and I laughed as we sped along the streets, both of us getting thoroughly drenched. What could be a better symbol of hope than fat, sparkling raindrops falling through rich, golden sunlight?

We soon arrived at the storage facility and found the stone within minutes. Its front face was badly damaged in the center, but the date at the top left corner had been identified by scholars—although, as it was written in old Burmese script, I had great difficulty deciphering it. The back face was in good condition, although timeworn, and there, in the middle of the first line, were the words Myanmar Pyay.

My quest was over.

CHAPTER NINE
Prelude in Bagan

Before my downriver trip to Pyay from Bagan, I had to stay for a few days in that old city of temples. I have been to Bagan many times before, but this trip was special. My schoolmates and I were going to attend a religious ceremony called kahtein, given by another schoolmate, Teddy Saing.

We were all alumni of the Methodist English High School, which we (as a matter of vanity) and others (as a matter of fact) consider the best high school in Myanmar. Products of a coeducational school with American roots, we were even in our teens a more sophisticated and on the whole a wilder bunch than the strictly protected and better-behaved students who grew up under the steely eyes of nuns and priests at the not-by-a-long-shot-coeducational Catholic missionary schools. (I think those students were not allowed to so much as mention the opposite sex.)

Our wildness gave us the ability to take risks as adults, and in a conservative society like Myanmar that put us some lengths ahead of the rest. There were in our school a number of nerds and a few extremely wild ones who fell by the wayside, but almost all of us are doing well and we still look out for each other.

We often go on holidays together, to the beach or to Pyay, a town six hours away by road, simply because we agree that this is where to find the best chicken curry and Indian paratas, or that Shwe Taung, the neighboring town, is the source of the best coconut cream noodles. It maddens my brother's class of '60, who are more serious, that we of '65 take trips in pursuit of food.

One evening at a party Teddy Saing, class of '66, announced that he would be holding a kahtein ceremony ten days from now in Bagan, and that anyone who cared to come would have free accommodations at his Kumudra Hotel.

A kahtein is a ceremony held in November, in which wooden frames called treasure trees are loaded with gifts that monks can use and are carried to a monastery to be distributed among its inhabitants. The ceremony can be a collective affair with gifts coming from markets, communities, schools, offices, or private individuals.

For Teddy's kahtein, Alan Kyaw Maung, who runs a travel company, booked twenty return tickets on the spot. I booked a one-way flight, planning to return on the river—but I kept that to myself. My school chums are not the type to approve of the boat which I wanted to take.

On the morning of our arrival in Bagan we were taken straight to a tea shop where a simple farmer's breakfast dish of rice mixed with oil had achieved a fame that had reached our ears in Yangon.

The tea shop was packed with locals and Burmese pilgrims. The appeal of this dish is due to the best oil obtained from peanuts crushed in a wooden mill turned by bovine power—not in a metal mill operated by electricity. Myanmar food purists insist on this wood-mill process; the resulting oil is more expensive but apparently worth the cost.

It was served with many side dishes: small chicken sausages like chopped-off pinkies, kimchi-like pickles, flaky deep-fried beef, tiny fish cakes, briny duck eggs, crisp omelettes, and other dishes. Soon our tables were piled with empty plates and we were driven off and settled into Teddy's hotel. We spent the rest of the day touring the ancient temples and buying piles of Bagan lacquerware. Shops selling all sorts of goods lined the walkways of the pagodas; I bought a light woolen blanket and a men's longyi of smooth blue cotton.

The next day, the guys set off at dawn for a round of golf and we "girls" drove to Mount Popa, abode of the spirits, particularly that of Popa Maidaw, the Mother Goddess of Popa.

Rosebud, my old classmate and my roommate during this trip, has a family tradition of paying homage to Min Maha Giri or the Lord of the Mountain, Guardian Spirit of the Home. She planned to offer the Kadaw Pwe, which is a green coconut placed between three bunches of green bananas and given in homage at the Lord of the Mountain's main shrine.

The drive to Popa through wooded hills and shady villages is always a pleasant one. Most of us opted to climb the thousand steps to the shrine, but I only went up halfway to browse in the shops lining the stairs. I saw pots of gamoun, wild plants from the orchid, ginger, and lily families that are considered medicinal or lucky, such as the one called Come Gold Come Silver. Another that is called the Butterfly had exotic flowers that looked not at all like butterflies but like floral spawns of the devil, almost evil, with large, dark purple flowers and whiskers hanging off its face. Bulbs of another gamoun looked like porcelain eggs, smooth and white. There were bunches of brown twigs with short leafless branches at one end, like dried fingers of a mummy, thin claws curled in the air as if grasping invisible necks.

My former classmate Liz and I strolled around the paved area that jutted off the side of the cliff, looking into more shops selling what is known as the "pagoda gem," clear agate imbedded with white bands that at times form the shape of a spire. We saw no one in the shop at first and were peering around when we heard someone from behind the curtain at the back calling to us, "Please, Aunties, will you share our lunch?"

It was the shopkeeper and his family asking us to share their food since we had turned up during their meal. We said thank you, we have eaten already, although if I had been alone I might have accepted, as I have done at times to the utter delight of strangers. But Liz would have killed me on the spot for violating what she considers decent social behavior—that you should not jump in and eat unless it's with someone you know.

I bought a few pagoda gems and a pair of matching moonstones for earrings. I like the story of the Popa Maidaw, a princess of the eleventh century who fell in love with a stranger from another land and later saw him and their two sons executed by the king they served. She is the guardian spirit of women everywhere and I wanted to have something to wear that came from her main shrine.

As we stopped to gaze out over the plains below us, a tiny baby monkey crawled to our feet and sat there looking up with beseeching eyes, mewing softly as a kitten. Babies of any species are heart-melting ... oh well, not tadpoles, I admit ... and we would have scooped this very small creature with very large eyes up into our arms, if Big Mama had not waddled up to give us a look: "I dare you."

We stood rooted to the spot, while a male monkey which looked like the big brother of the baby marched right up to me and peed on the bottom edge of my longyi. At that moment I could only reflect that my elder brother had never protected me in this manner. The family walked off in triumph while Liz nearly choked to death laughing at my new perfume.

I sat relaxing on one of the concrete seats that lined the steps while Liz bought some necklaces made of seeds. A gentlemanly monkey came to sit at my side, nibbling peanuts from a plastic bag with obvious enjoyment. All thoughts of relaxation vanished and with terror chilling my blood, I sat very still, hoping fervently that he would not offer to share his snack. Liz hissed from a safe distance that we made a charming couple and I dared not even scowl at her; all my muscles had gone as rigid as steel.

The next morning we were up and dressed to the nines for the kahtein ceremony: women in silks and long scarves, and men in neat jackets, silk longyi, and black velvet slippers. Beaming like a happy bear, rotund Teddy waddled up and down, inspecting the long lines of bullock carts with a treasure tree on each, hung with boxes that contained robes, umbrellas, towels, medicine, slippers, alms bowls, soap, fruit juice bottles, and other useful items for the monks. Crisp new cash notes had been folded and pinned into shapes of flowers and birds; these pretty things took pride of place at the tip of the frames.

Rosebud and I gingerly climbed onto the back of a cart, sitting backward with our silk-clad legs dangling off the edge. We held on

tightly to the sides to keep from sliding off onto the dusty road just in case the cart climbed a hill. The hitched oxen wore silk flowers on their heads, with red velvet harnesses decorated with gold thread, mirrored circlets, and tiny bells. Long strings of colourful pom-poms were wrapped around their bodies. The looks in their eyes seemed to ask, "Dammit, is it this time of the year again?"

We were off with a jerk of the reins and wild cries from the village kids who bounded into the road. They scampered in the dust and I saw Teddy walking some distance in front of the procession, throwing wrapped candy from a silver bowl. The night before I had seen his family wrap folded cash notes in candy wrappers and mix them with pieces of real candy. This is the part of religious celebrations when "gold" and "silver" rain on the people.

Led by a loud walking band playing the traditional instruments of drum, bamboo clappers, cymbals, and oboe, we arrived at a monastery on the bank of the Ayeyarwaddy River, and Teddy and his family disappeared inside with the offerings. We knew there would be a sermon and some rituals for them to observe, so the rest of us walked over to chairs set under a spreading tree on the riverbank. There we hungrily waited for lunch, which would not arrive until the monks had been served.

When lunch came, spread on long tables under shady trees, we bent our heads to it. There was rice, chicken and pork curries with the pork cooked for hours so it melted in our mouths, huge sweet river prawns in gravy rich with tomatoes and tomalley, tart vegetable soup, vegetable salads, bamboo shoots fried with shrimp, and large dishes of the best tomato-and-salted-fish relish we had ever eaten in our lives.

Afterward we went to tour more temples but this time, bloated with food, at a slower pace. At dinner that night we demanded more of the tomato relish. Then I tottered off to bed while the "boys" began a karaoke session as they often do at our parties, reviving the songs of our early teens. As Victor Chit began to warble the first lines of Paul Anka's "Diana" ... "I'm so young and you're so old oh my darling I've been told" ... I thought to myself, Now that I'm very much no longer sixteen, I no longer like that song.

Early the next morning I was packed and all ready to take the kind of small cargo boat that is used by market women. Ma Maw, the wife of my publisher, had an office in Bagan and she sent her car to take me to the jetty. The driver brought my ticket that Ma Maw had purchased the previous day. He also brought an armload of snacks that she had sent "to eat on the way." (Burmese travelers always carry loads of food when they travel, as if they were going to cross the Sahara, and their friends make sure that they will never starve to death even if they are only going on an hour's drive.)

My other friends were still sleeping when I said goodbye to my roommate, Rosebud. She reminded me not to forget that the night before I had promised everyone that I would eat, on their behalf, the fish with oyster sauce in Pyay at the Mingalar Garden Hotel. I assured her I could never forget anything to do with food; it is simply not in my mental makeup.

I looked around the small jetty with a few restaurants and general stores and settled myself into a combination of both, run

by a couple of young women who looked like sisters. I ordered tea and ei kya kwei, puffy deep-fried dough sticks, and sat enjoying my breakfast while a dog with a fluffy tail snored at my feet under the table. The tablecloth was worn but freshly starched and pressed. A huge tamarind tree with a deep brown trunk and pale green leaves hovered over the roof, giving cool shade and a crisp freshness to the slightly chilly early-morning air.

The girls told me that the boat would come from Pakokku, a few miles upriver, but because the port authorities there were holding their kahtein ceremony today I might have to wait a few hours. They brought me newspapers, a fan, and a dish of pickled tea leaves. I bought a packet of biscuits and two bottles of water and tucked them into my bag.

Resigned to my fate, I settled back in a comfortable chair, and prepared to make friends with my hostesses.

As it was only about 9 a.m. there were few customers apart from a child or two. One boy came to buy an ice-lolly.

"It's still early and cold, so why are you buying an ice-lolly?" Graceful Bright asked the kid as she took out one from the icebox to give him. "You'll get a sore throat, you will. I'll tell your mother if you come again." She slapped the money into a tin box and slammed the lid.

A few minutes later a girl in her teens came to buy some pickled plums, holding the hand of a barefooted toddler.

"Now don't go giving any of these green plums to the baby, you hear?" I heard one sister say to the teenager. "And look here, the ground is so cold and there's nothing on the baby's feet. Do you even notice it's winter?"

November with the temperature in the thirties is what we call winter.

"Go put some socks on her feet, or carry her," she called after them. The older girl laughed, picked up the baby, tucking her on one hip with an expert flip, and ambled away with the plastic bag of red plums clenched between her lips. The baby, in spite of a grimy face, was fair-skinned and very pretty, with curly brown hair and huge, melting eyes. Surely, the gangly teenager with thick eyebrows could not be her relative.

Pretty Bright leaned close to me and whispered, "The baby was given away; it was so tragic."

Given away? A baby? I was instantly intrigued.

"About two years back, someone got off the cargo boat, the small one you're taking today, Aunty. She came from Pakokku or perhaps a village near there or even further upriver."

A young woman with reddened eyes had come ashore holding a baby who was only a few days old.

"She just walked around the jetty, asking if anyone would please take her child and bring her up. She didn't say anything else, gave no explanation but she said she was seventeen years old when someone asked. She didn't answer when a woman asked her what happened."

The young mother had begun to sob as a crowd gathered, silently staring at her with pity.

"Aunty, you see that noodle shop over there?" She pointed to a long table set out in the open very near the river; the table was covered with a plastic sheet and there were bottles, pots, and bowls stacked on it. A wooden bench ran along its front.

"The couple who runs it already had four kids but they took the baby. The poor young woman, she was so pretty ... she left by the next upriver boat."

She had stood on deck looking back at her baby, fast asleep in the arms of her new mother.

"Tears were just pouring down her face, like rain. Now no one can even mention the story in front of that couple, they get so mad for fear that the child will hear of it. The whole family adores this little thing. We never saw her mother again."

People from the towns and villages on the river knew each other, I was sure. Perhaps the mother often asked others if they had seen her baby on their trips to Nyaung Oo. Pilgrims often came to Bagan by boat, especially during the annual festivals of the bigger temples when tens of thousands of people gather, such festivals being country fairs to trade and buy goods. Maybe she came sometimes, hidden in the crowds, to secretly look over at the noodle shop?

I stared at the baby, now with thick woolen booties on her little feet, giggling as her father held her up and blew bubbles on her dusty little tummy.

"Your boat's coming!" Hla Hla Win cried. "Take your time, Aunty, passengers must get down first."

The small, grimy-looking little vessel was still some way off. On the roof right at the front there was something black and bulky. As the boat got nearer, I saw that it was the papier-mâché head and body, now in two separate pieces, of a "dancing elephant" from Kyaukse, another town just south of Mandalay. Their annual October festival, a competition for men dancing inside life-sized elephant figures, has become very popular all over the country as entertainment for ceremonies. This troupe had apparently performed in Pakokku and they seemed to have another gig in Bagan, for men were getting ready to carry the elephant off the boat.

A boy jumped into the restaurant to grab my bag and I said goodbye to the sisters.

I remember them still, their upright figures and serene faces, true daughters of the central plains. The dry heat and harsh weather of Bagan produce strong and dignified people, and the ancient temples exude an air of tranquility in which people's spirits thrive.

CHAPTER TEN
On the Cargo Boat

The small cargo boat chugged and shuddered to the riverbank with impatient passengers lining the rails. I could see by their faces that they were ready to leap ashore. The grimy, dilapidated boat looked as though it were held together with duct tape but its small size, plus its furiously smoking chimney and growling engine, gave it an air of bravado like a scruffy and smelly little terrier swaggering up to fight a bigger dog.

Porters hurried to grab the outward end of the gangplank, pulling it up to the bank, and passengers practically galloped off, lugging baskets and cardboard boxes. The boy carrying my bag leaped aboard as soon as the last passenger had one foot on the ground.

I followed gingerly, and then a man in the water held up his hand for me to hold as he walked alongside. (Oh how I adore men who help me walk the plank.) Thanking him with a smile, I jumped onto the lower deck, which was packed with towering stacks of baskets that held wooden clogs, betel nuts, semidry tobacco leaves, and small terra-cotta cooking pots packed in straw. Several families had managed to squeeze in as well.

I gave my name and showed my ticket to one harried-looking man who seemed in charge. He bellowed into the engine room and a wiry, shirtless young man covered in soot climbed up through an opening and gestured for me to follow him.

We went up a narrow metal stairway to the upper deck, which was also crowded with people. He led me to a narrow space between two women, took my bag from the boy, and dumped it there. He left, still without a word, while I settled down.

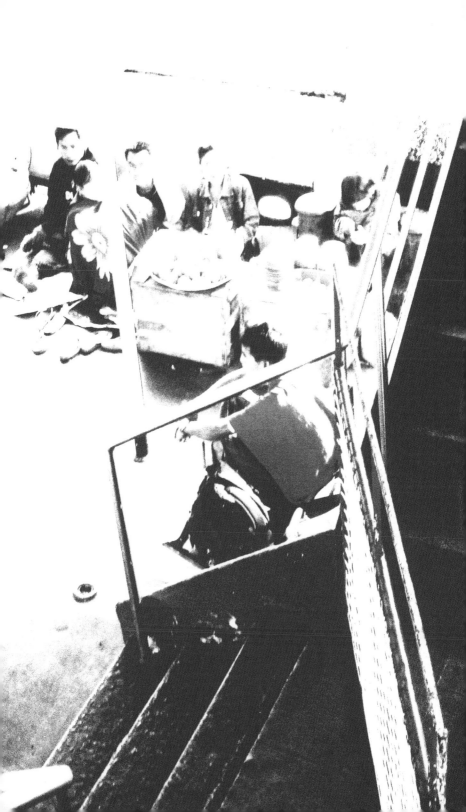

That is, I took out a plastic sheet I had brought from Yangon from my bag, spread it over the iron deck that was gritty with sand, and laid out the light woolen blanket I had just bought in Bagan. Over that I put my newly purchased longyi, which I could use as a blanket to cover my feet for decency's sake when I was lying down. I took out the bottles of drinking water, the biscuits, and a small plastic bag for garbage. My now-softer bag was the pillow. I was done preparing my "berth" in less than three minutes.

I sat back and looked around, with my feet tucked under me and covered with my longyi. On my right were a thin, elderly woman and her daughter, who seemed to be in her twenties. They had a tall basket near them packed with straw hats and another filled with strips of straw. They sat with busy fingers, weaving three straws into flat ribbons that would later be sewn by machine into hats.

The daughter had a smooth, clear, and dark complexion, her face a perfect soft oval with a high-bridged nose, flaring eyebrows, and sparkling black eyes. She smiled ever so slightly. Her eyes danced with warmth when she glanced up at me before thick lashes hid her eyes as she bent to her work. Her mother studied me shyly out of the corner of her eye while she wove the straws.

Directly across and against the railings, with a narrow aisle between the bottom of our "berths" and theirs, sat two diminutive women with a little plate of pickled tea leaves and two small cups of green tea resting between them. On either side of them were baskets, one filled with a flask, a stacked tiffin carrier, bottles of water, and two woolen sweaters. Another basket was filled with sections of thanakha logs, that fragrant, expensive wood, and the thick cotton blankets of Pakokku that are so highly prized throughout the country. I later found out that they, Daw Tint Sein, "Ms. Elegant Diamond" and Daw Htay, "Ms. Wealthy," had been buying stock for their general store in their hometown of Myanaung, a name that always sounds like a cat's sweet cry to me.

The mother making hats was Daw Win Kyi, "Ms. Bright and Clear." She and her eighteen-year-old daughter Ei Ei Htwe, "Soft Soft Youngest," both lived in a village near the town of Myinmu.

My companions and I sat in silence, eyeing each other in a friendly way. Gradually, as I plastered a shy, sweet smile on my face (the look that used to alert my father that I was up to something), they felt I should be made "at home" and began a conversation that included me. Half an hour into their chatter, I felt as though I were in a 1950s Burmese novel.

The conversation between Ms. Elegant Diamond and Ms. Wealthy glittered with idioms and proverbs that I had often heard when growing up. They had vanished from urban speech a long time ago, replaced by modern slang that has no poetry; now the only times I can still enjoy these quirky phrases are in books set in the '50s. It was the language of our rural community—not only the words but the subjects—gossip about sex, for example.

But not explicit or innuendo-laden references to the sexual act. It was about the scandalous behaviour of sexual misconduct—girls and boys holding hands in the street or a woman with her hand on the arm of her husband. They had seen such instances in Pakokku and now asked each other what on earth the world was coming to.

"Doesn't the girl know that if they break up after letting everyone see her holding hands like that it's her reputation that will suffer? After all, 'if the leaf falls on the thorn or the thorn falls on the leaf,' it's the leaf that will be damaged, not the thorn."

"Well, maybe she thought it's all right to have 'a thousand boyfriends but one husband'? Remember that woman in the market, wearing that yellow batik longyi, remember how she was clutching her husband's arm and letting him hold their baby? People like that, older ones, set a bad example for the young girls."

"If a woman has a faithful husband, she's lucky but you know what they say, 'men like to wash their feet at every puddle they see';

men think that 'all noble men deserve a thousand wives.'"

"If they are noble; that saying was for heroes like Anawrahta or Kyansittha. Who nowadays are like them?"

"Now then, what about your old man? You know he doesn't even dare glance at other women."

The other did not reply as she puffed on her cheroot but gave a look to her friend full of mischief, smugness, and a hint of "just let him try."

I'd bet anything their husbands keep away from all puddles in their path.

On the other side Soft Youngest was reassuring her mother that her younger sister was "only friends" with her classmate, son of the village grocer.

"She's good in math and he's good in history, and they help each other with their notes," she was saying to Mother Bright and Clear. "They don't even meet outside of school, they just exchange notebooks."

"Well, 528 can easily turn into 1500," her mother warned. (528 is the symbol for platonic love or that between family and relatives, while 1500 is sexual. I have no idea if the numbers are from lists such as in "How do I love thee? Let me count the ways ... ")

Mother Bright continued in a testy voice, "Why didn't you tell me before they were exchanging books? Next time check them, there might be love letters tucked into them."

Rural houses have no phones because they are expensive, and country women do not hang out in cafés or tea shops (as they are only beginning to do in towns, since, hooray! We are now in the twenty-first century!), so a boy who wants to declare his love usually passes a note hidden in a book. To give the letter openly to the girl or to actually tell her in public would insult her—and she would never be allowed to go out alone, anyway. He cannot use the post, for the mother would open every single letter that comes for her daughters.

(Forget the Rights of Personal Privacy when they come up against the Rights of Mum.)

Hiding notes in books, bribing the postman, or using best friends as couriers are the boy's safest bets, as is riding his bike past her house, a hundred times a day if possible, choosing the times when her mother is away.

He might also play his guitar and sing from a distance—close enough that his beloved could hear him but not loud enough that her vigilant mother would send the girl's father or brothers after him. Not that her mother would have anything against the boy per se, but it's a tradition to protect daughters as if they were "enclosed in seven iron cages." If all went well, after the wedding her mum would try to get him to be a member of her family while his mum would do the same thing to her new daughter-in-law.

I thought I would check out the food and sanitation facilities before dinnertime. On the lower deck right at the stern there were two toilets, both with chipped tiles but clean. The ledge between them that opened out to the river was apparently the bathroom, for a woman was bathing her young son with river water that she pulled up in a pail that was tied to the boat. She was clad only in a longyi tucked up under her armpits and over her breasts, so it looked as though she would be bathing after she was done with the buck-naked little boy, who squirmed like a lathered eel under her vigorously scrubbing hands.

I came back upstairs again, making my careful way through people who sat gossiping in groups, no doubt making comments on how the daring young couples of today hold hands in the streets. On our deck at the stern there was a plastic-covered table with small stools around it, one side manned by a man in a grimy sweatshirt. A rusty fridge stood behind him, its body wrapped with an iron chain locked at the front with an equally rusty padlock. It looked like a captured, unhealthy alien that was being held prisoner.

There were three or four battered aluminum pots in front of the attendant with a stack of porcelain plates next to them. I asked what curries he had and he opened the lids with a flourish. There was egg curry with halved hard-boiled eggs cooked in a spicy gravy, there was a stew of vegetable and chickpeas, there was a mixture of wilted, overcooked vegetables, and there was pork curry, with hog hairs still sprouting out of the thick rinds. I hate wilted vegetables, loathe hard-boiled eggs, and have never liked chickpeas. *And* I could make a sizable paint brush if I collected the hog hairs in the pot of pork. I thought I could make do with the snacks I'd brought with me—while inwardly I writhed in agony at the thought—or would buy food at whatever stops we made on the way. But Ei Ei Htwe had warned me that because our boat was delayed, the timing of stops would be off and hawkers might not be waiting at the jetties.

The two ladies across from me knew I had been checking out the food stall, deducing it from my lack of a tiffin carrier and perhaps my perpetually hungry look. They said I must eat with them because the food stall on board was too dirty and too expensive, and I accepted gratefully.

Later that day I asked my comrades where I could get a bucket on a string, because I wanted a bath. I was told that the one at the stern was for all passengers to use, but that because it was dark I would probably catch a chill if I bathed now. I reassured them I was used to bathing at all hours, and that this was a good time since nobody else would want to use the bucket. I decorously pulled a cotton longyi up to my chin like a tent and removed my T-shirt, bra, and the longyi that I had been wearing. I tied the fresh cotton longyi under my armpits and wrapped a large towel around my shoulders so that they would not be shamelessly naked. From chin to ankles I was totally and decently covered and could now go down to the lower deck, carrying my soap dish and the longyi I had been wearing.

The bucket was free and the water was icy cold and brown

with mud, but very refreshing. I bathed wearing the longyi, then changed into the dry one I'd worn earlier, wrung out the wet one, and walked back to my berth where I wrapped my wet longyi in a plastic bag.

When my neighbors discovered I had not brought along a stone mortar and thanakha log so I could grind fresh paste to smear on my face, they brought out their mortar, which they had wrapped in a clean cloth, and lent me a section of thanakha log. I would have been utterly disgraced to have a bare, oily face in public so I sprinkled a few drops of water on the stone surface, ground the side of the small log over it in a few swipes, and rubbed my face with the thin paste. It smelled wonderful; filthy rich these ladies may not have been, but their thanakha came from the Shinma Taung region and was both the best and the most expensive.

After sunset Ei Ei Htwe was still weaving straw. Her mother sat facing in the direction where her head would be if she were lying down, a rope of the 108 Buddhist beads in her hand, praying softly as her fingers dropped each bead.

I asked Ei Ei Htwe about the hats and she said the straw was from wheat stalks, which are flexible and have a lovely golden color with a sheen. She showed me how to fold and turn and tuck in the ends to add to the length, and I picked up a few straws and began.

"We used to farm when Father was alive," she told me as we worked. "I don't have brothers, so after he died we sold the farm and Mother bought a store. My married older sister runs it, she lives with us. Mother and I make hats and sell them at the pagoda festivals. We're on our way to to Pyay's Shwe Sandaw Pagoda festival."

"How do these strips get sewn? Do you do it yourself?" I asked, curious about the final process.

"My elder sister sews them sometimes, or I do when I'm home, or my youngest sister when she's free from homework. We bought an old sewing machine last year."

She fell silent for a moment.

"I failed matriculation. It was the year Father died and I didn't want to go back to school. But our youngest will get a degree and be a high school teacher. She's very smart, she could be a doctor but we can't afford that."

Medical school is seven years' work and although school fees are not high compared to other countries, private dorms and food can be expensive. At times the community will chip in to send a poor student with high marks to med school, but I had no idea if Ei Ei Htwe's village or township could do that. I told her there are private foundations that might provide funds and that her sister should try to get the best marks that she could achieve.

The boat docked for the night and dinner was served. We feasted on rice and dry-cooked chicken heart, liver, and stomach, aromatic with garlic. There were pickled tea leaves and fried peanuts, snacks that go well with rice. With two of us using empty sections of the carrier and the other using the upturned cover, we each had "plates." They would not hear of me taking the cover—I was their guest, after all.

From a plastic box there came grilled shrimp paste pounded with green chillies and sprinkled lavishly with lime juice. There was enough oil from the chicken liver dish to dribble on our rice, and how I loved the chewy texture and taste of the stomach.

After dinner I offered to wash up but my hostesses protested, saying it was easier for them since they were sitting right against the rails. They washed with a little water from their bottle and carefully flung away the used water so that it wouldn't land on the deck downstairs.

I turned my ears again to eavesdrop on our neighbors across the aisle. They were chatting about a wealthy woman in their neighborhood whose son had died about a year ago and who asked a famous spirit medium to tell her where her son had been reborn.

"Well, well! It seems that the son, who was killed in a drunken brawl, was reborn as a calf, born to one of U Po Thone's cows, you know that grouchy, ugly old man who lives at the south end of the village, near the primary school?"

Apparently the mother had bought the calf from that mean old man, who had asked a bundle for it.

"No wonder her son became an animal," one lady said to the other. "Remember the time he was so rude to Granny Aye Bon, and even swore at her? That's what happens to people who insult elders."

The other said, "That old man ripped her off, but then she could afford it. It's her fault, you know, she spoilt her son so he became a drunk. Now she's keeping the calf like a king."

"Spoilt her son when he was a human and now she's spoiling him as a calf. I hope the poor animal won't grow up to be a drunk."

They giggled like schoolgirls.

For a while people had gone to inspect the calf and to listen to the mother's teary tale, but within a few days people forgot all about it.

"Well, as they say, 'praise lasts seven days and criticism lasts seven days,' and so it is with something like this," one said to the other.

By 9 p.m., we were all "in bed," after everyone else had said their prayers—I forgot. But I did not forget to go to the food stall before I went to bed to give the grimy man some money, telling him to get me one large chicken cut in medium pieces and deep-fry it by lunchtime the next day.

The boat left our overnight stop early the next morning. Hawkers were selling breakfast before we cast off. When I woke up, I saw that some families on the bathing deck were already cooking rice on small charcoal stoves. Kids ran among the packed passengers, screaming and chasing each other. A family huddled in a corner, the father handing out biscuits to two toddlers while the mother poured them weak coffee in tea mugs; it's not unusual for Myanmar children to grow up drinking milky tea or coffee.

I stopped a girl who carried a basket of steaming sticky rice on her head. She removed the clean cotton cloth covering the food and sold me six packets of steamed rice with soft beans, liberally garnished with shredded coconut. I shared it with my berth mates, who first declined out of politeness until I said that, pig as I was, I still could not eat all of it. I have never eaten any sticky rice that good—soft and sweet, with nutty, savory beans and creamy coconut shreds.

At lunchtime I fetched my fried chicken and passed it around, but I had to insist before my companions would agree to share it with me. I ate again with the ladies opposite me, whose rice was freshly cooked and warm. I found out that they paid a family on the lower deck, friends from their hometown, to cook extra rice for them. The heart and liver curry of the day before was more delicious than ever. They had also prepared a tomato relish, having asked their friends below to grill some tomatoes on the charcoal fire, which were then peeled and mashed with chopped green chillies, thinly sliced raw onions, and fish sauce. The fried chicken was tender, thank God—by the size of it, which I could guess earlier when I had seen the pieces wrapped in a newspaper, I'd thought it would be a grandfather rooster and tough as leather.

As the day wore on, I was dying to lie down but no one else was. It would be indecent to be prone in public so I, used to flopping into bed when I am not at my desk, gritted my teeth and sat leaning against my bag, chatting to Ei Ei Htwe and weaving straw. I finally gave up because my back was killing me. I forever disgraced myself in the eyes of my neighbors by tumbling on my side, curled up like a fetus and covering myself, especially my feet, with the man's longyi I was using as a blanket. Lying flat on my back would have been too,

too disgraceful, showing my "front" in a prostrate position for all to see. It was somewhat better to be curled up.

After dinner that night, Ei Ei Htwe and I sat talking softly. She gently probed to learn what I did for a living and I told her I lived in Yangon and was a writer. When she said it must be "comfortable" work "in the shade," I said although it was not manual labor, it was hard work, with my head feeling as if it were right in the open, under the sunlight, with no umbrella. She laughed and said that before, when they had the farm, all of her family members had to work "under the sun"; now that it was sold, it was tiring to sit for hours weaving straw but at least it was "in the shade."

The next day, soon after we left, I heard the ladies across the aisle exclaim, their voices joined by other passengers, "There's Let Pan Village! There's Maha Peinné Pagoda! See, it was at the Maha Peinné Festival over there, where Shwe Mann Tin Maung died, right there onstage."

They continued to talk about this man, and with my eyes closed I could hear the longing in their voices, as well as the joy, as they relived his plays and songs all over again. They were regular travelers on this route, but I was certain that every time they passed this town they honored the memory of the dancer who was one of the greatest luminaries of the Zat theater.

In spite of the many video halls that have spread throughout the country, Burmese people still enjoy performances of the Zat traditional theater, which begins at around 9 p.m. and goes on all night. Before an intermission at about 2 a.m. there are concerts, an operetta, and dances performed in groups or in duets. After a half-hour break, the final presentation—a long classical play—goes on until dawn.

Shwe Mann Tin Maung was a star performer in the Zat theater from the mid-1930s up until his death in 1969. His heart was not strong but despite the protests of his family he had insisted on

continuing to perform, and he died as he would have wanted. Millions of his fans mourned his passing and still do; no other Zat star has ever been as well loved as he was.

I had met him once years ago. That was the night that his shy and beautiful nineteen-year-old son Win Bo made his debut. My seventeen-year-old heart fluttered at the son's good looks and my senses reeled with the impact of the father's splendor and grace.

The Zat theater tradition has now declined into the shame of the audience preferring the lead dancers to do rock or rap concerts instead of classical plays. Shwe Mann Tin Maung's younger sons Win Maung and Chan Thar, who once danced in a troupe, now live and work in New York where they teach dance. When they perform in Yangon on their visits I try not to miss their shows; words cannot describe their melting grace. Sadly, Win Bo, the hero of my youth, is now bedridden with ill health.

As we neared Pyay, I gave my wool blanket to a poor family on the lower deck and packed up my things. Ei Ei Htwe took my little plastic bag of rubbish that I had carefully kept safe for two and a half days so that I could discard it on land, and threw it into the river. I shrieked and told her fish could eat the plastic and die.

"No, they won't," she retorted. "Fish are not that dumb."

Ah well. I did not want to lecture her on keeping our rivers clean; it would make me sound patronizing.

We docked in Pyay at dusk and I said tender goodbyes to everyone, especially young Ei Ei Htwe. My traveling companions waved from the deck as I climbed the steps, watched as I flagged down a trishaw, and continued to wave as I rode away.

I asked the trishaw peddler to take me to book a bus ticket, and he did, gently lecturing me about the dangers of a woman going about alone in the dark of evening. I knew I was perfectly safe, not only with him but under any circumstances, because street violence in my country at any hour is very rare.

He dropped me off at the Mingalar Garden Hotel, my favorite place in Pyay, with another warning not to be so "daring" next time. I thanked him gratefully, tipped him well, and staggered into the lobby, disheveled and somewhat grubby.

After the receptionists welcomed me with open arms, I took a Japanese-style room, had a hot shower, and ate fish in oyster sauce. I wrote about the last three days until late that night, thinking about Ei Ei Htwe, little Soft Youngest, and wishing her a life of being "in the shade."

PART III
The Delta

CHAPTER ELEVEN
Disaster

On May 2, 2008, before I could explore the Ayeyarwaddy delta, Cyclone Nargis swept over it with winds of 150 miles per hour. It was the worst natural disaster Myanmar has ever suffered, with tens of thousands of people and whole villages washed away by the tidal wave. Warnings were given, but few, including me, took notice, as we thought the storm would be over in two hours, tops. It lasted for more than twelve.

That evening, I was still out on the streets after dark, driving back home in the lashing rain but feeling unconcerned. As I waited for traffic lights to change, a young girl, her head barely reaching my window, came around with a few strings of jasmine flowers for sale. Usually I never hang garlands from the rearview mirror as others do, since I'm afraid that their to-and-fro swing might hypnotize me and make me crash, but this girl was soaked through and through. Water was running down her head and face as if someone were pouring a bucketful over her. I handed her a 1000-kyat note, but before she could untangle the wet strings from her fingers the lights changed and I drove off, fluttering my fingers in goodbye through the window.

She shrieked after me in this shrill, child's voice: "Aunteee! Your floweers!"

I can still hear her.

Previously I had not traveled much in the delta, where so much rice is grown that we call it the rice bowl of the country. My ancestors were from the dry and hot Upper Myanmar region. I grew up in Yangon, the capital city since 1885 and only recently usurped by the new capital of Naypyidaw, a word which in fact means "capital city" and is also used in our language to say, for example, "London is the Naypyidaw of the United Kingdom."

Although Yangon is in the delta, unlike the delta proper it has no streams and creeks running in its vicinity like the strands of a spider's web. I knew that villagers in the delta use boats more than they do bikes or carts or cars, and my trepidation at the sight of shaky gangplanks has stopped me from exploring the area on my own. But when I started this book, I thought it would be a good chance to see this fertile and green land, to paddle along twisting creeks past twisted mangrove roots. I had looked forward to traveling along one of the nine rivulets that branch out from the Ayeyarwaddy as it rushes toward the Bay of Bengal. I wanted to go to Pyapon for its annual folk theater and to Mawtin Zun, the very tip of the curly western edge of Myanmar that looks out toward the Indian Ocean.

Twanté is one town in the delta I visit regularly. It is the old City of Pots mentioned in seventh-century stone tablets from the Pyu Kingdom of Srikhetera. As it is not far from Yangon, it was not difficult to visit the potteries there, which still use old technology to produce shining, black-glazed pots, from tiny toy cups to mid-sized ones to store soft fish paste to the huge bulbous Martaban jars, rounded at the top like an egg and standing on a tapering bottom, which is to be buried in the ground for balance.

I have often walked over the empty fields outside of Twanté, eyes scanning the ground for bits of celadon. We no longer produce this, but scholars have discovered about a thousand old kilns all over the delta and beautiful shards of green or green-on-white can still be found, as well as bits that are black or brown. I once came upon a fragment with shallow lines that meandered downward, filled with glistening brown glaze that flowed down the lines like muddy water; it seemed to represent the delta's many waterways.

Just four months after finding that piece I was riding on a boat in the delta along meandering muddy creeks, while rain fell steadily on my head. I was helping friends take relief goods to those villages in Yangon Division that had been destroyed by Cyclone Nargis.

By the time Nargis faded, huge areas of the delta were left devastated. In many places the tidal wave had erased all traces of people, cattle, children, houses. The government held meetings and arranged rescue and relief, while international organizations and governments rallied to help.

Meanwhile many people of Yangon, somewhat still in shock but knowing there were victims worse off than they, began to go out in small groups three or four days after the cyclone to see what could be done for the people of the delta.

An expatriate friend, Gill, who owns the upscale River Art Gallery and is a member of a social welfare group, was also collecting relief goods. At one point she had stored several bags of rice in her gallery situated inside the elegant and extremely expen-

sive Strand Hotel. One hotel guest had wandered in and, looking in appreciation at the pile of rice bags, asked her the price of this "installation" and when it could be shipped to Texas. Beautiful Gill, honest woman that she is, did not take the opportunity to generate a hefty sum for relief work, whereas I would have been quite prepared to lie, cheat, or steal to help the victims. (Luckily, friends I e-mailed came to the rescue so I did not have to commit any felonies.)

Convoys of trucks from the business community went into the delta; they also lent the government heavy machinery to clear away the fallen trees and electric power poles. Famous monks traveled all over the country to preach and collect millions of kyat to buy supplies.

At first there was some political standoff between donors from Western governments and Myanmar's military government, the former politicizing the situation with calls for a regime change, and the latter, already xenophobic to the nth degree, refusing to allow U.S. ships to dock and Marines to disembark at Yangon's port.

The world feared that if no international relief teams arrived with help, tens of thousands of storm victims would die of starvation or disease. They were not aware that local people who were rich and those who were not at all were dipping into their savings (without a tax break option) to donate to relief efforts, and that those who had only a little shared with those who had even less. This was not a one-time thing occurring only after Nargis; throughout our history when a part of a town has been devastated by fire or other calamities, people rally to donate food or goods of their own volition.

One effective Burmese NGO is made up mostly of intelligentsia who since 2000 have offered free funeral services. Now they branched out into the collection and donation of goods. Being unable to have a decent funeral is a great loss of face for the deceased person's family, and this organization filled a much-needed niche. They were already well-known throughout the country, with branch offices in many towns, and they managed to do a lot of good in this disaster.

Monks collected vast amounts of funds and provided manpower through their thousands of devotees. Movie stars, publishers, and popular musicians went out with huge amounts of relief supplies. Private companies met with the government and took responsibility to help various sections of the delta.

I found out that a couple who is like my family had been running goods to some devastated areas around the small town of Kunchangon. They had not informed me, since they knew that I do not have much to give and were reluctant to bother me for funds. The wife, Ma Hlaing, and her husband, Kyaw, run a small furniture business. The roof of their storage building next to where they live blew off during the cyclone but, they explained, their goods were not perishable so they suffered no loss.

(Ma Hlaing and I had met under ... let's say, stressful circumstances about twenty years ago, and her great sense of humor eased a lot of our discomfort during that time.)

They had calculated how much they would have lost if their furniture inventory had been destroyed, and decided to donate the equal amount to those who had fared worse. They dipped into their savings and when that was not enough, Kyaw sold his wife's gold bangles. "He's not going to drink it away or gamble," Ma Hlaing said; "so that's fine by me."

By then they had exhausted their resources and gone way beyond their budget but felt they needed to do more. Ma Hlaing made a base at a monastery in Kunchangon. She knew that the abbot was very kind, had a large network of followers, and could tell her which village was in need of what, how long it would take to reach it by car or boat, and how many households were there. He could also arrange transportation. Sometimes he would call ahead to Yangon so that Ma Hlaing could arrange to send goods that would meet existing needs.

In one village they had given rice seeds, but only to about ten households since they did not have enough funds to buy seeds for all. The idea was that half the reaped paddy would go to the growers and half would be distributed to the other households. However, the whole village decided to give the half earmarked for the other families to be used to repair the crown of their pagoda that was damaged by the storm.

Schools had been destroyed but the government and the business community supplied large tents to use until they could be rebuilt. Monasteries had spacious halls for communal prayer or meditation so these were used for classes. And in a country where bamboo grows wild in abundance, even large shelters were easy to construct in a day, although the bamboo had to be brought in from undamaged areas.

As soon as I heard of Ma Hlaing's effort, I sent off an SOS to a few close friends, who sent me substantial donations although they were also giving quite a bit to larger organizations. By that time Ma Hlaing's small group had already made seven trips in their truck, at times renting another when the rice bags and other supplies were too much for one vehicle to carry.

On my first trip eighteen days after the storm we had driven through mud and barely discernible tracks to Kamar Kanaw, a village where it was impossible to go any farther by truck. All along the way we saw nature desecrated: trees bare of leaves, palm trees with their trunks and crowns all swayed to one side, broken trees, mud and debris everywhere.

While Kyaw and I stayed back at Kamar Kanaw to distribute rice and clothing, Ma Hlaing, three young doctors, and forty bags of rice traveled on two tractors to three villages farther away. There were so many people hanging from, and clinging to, the tractor that it looked like a moving mass of arms and heads and legs.

I met an orphan, a boy of seventeen who had watched helplessly as his parents and sister were washed away while he clung to a palm tree. Kyaw offered to take him to Yangon and find work for him there, or a job overseas, but he was adamant. He refused to leave his village, where only four huts were left out of thirty. He would continue to work the land.

On another trip we donated plastic sheets to use as roofs or walls; the monsoon season would soon be upon us and lashing rains would sweep the country. At least with rain, people would have clean water to drink, but shelter, food, and essentials like pots, clothing, and blankets were urgently needed.

On the road there were hundreds of similar groups every day; on weekends they were bumper-to-bumper. In Yangon everyone I know was chipping in what they could: my fashionable school chums went through their overflowing wardrobes and donated clothes, withdrew cash from fat bank accounts, and bought rice bags and cooking oil to send out through people like Ma Hlaing. In the early days many of the men driving out to these areas came back naked except for their underwear because they had given away everything else they were wearing.

The third time I went I brought 250 plastic pails with covers because the monsoon was really here by then and people needed something to store the rainfall. We also gave small but useful items like needles and thread, nail clippers, safety pins, gas lighters, plastic cups, and bowls, all packed in 250 individual bags.

Ma Hlaing and I were to stop at Kyar Kike, "Tiger Bites," Village, while her husband would go farther to villages closer to the sea. The drive to Tawku Village, from where we would take boats, was on a horrendously bad and narrow road covered with rocks that jutted out like broken teeth; we saw the reason why when about halfway along our route we came across a road roller lying on its side like an unwieldy yellow bug. It was so heavy that apparently no one could move it and it was beginning to rust.

After covering a distance of nine miles in one hour, we entered prosperous Tawku Village, where inhabitants own acres of paddy fields and are prosperous even by urban standards. Their neat and, by now, repaired houses lined both sides of "main street," with debris-laden fields as the backyards. Just two places were not yet repaired: the school with its roof missing and the police station represented only by a sign board propped against the gate of a cleared plot. The five-foot-long "jetty" of Tawku at the far end of the long main street was only a muddy, shallow bank. A shrine of a guardian Nat took up space on one side; on the other was the wall of a small house.

On our first trip here, I had seen our young doctors calmly peel fat, blood-filled leeches from their toes after standing in this sort of mud. I steeled myself not to shriek and run around like a chicken with its head cut off should I spot one feasting on my feet.

Kyar Kike villagers were waiting for us in two narrow, small paddle boats, and we hired bigger ones to carry the supplies. Due to the floods we could barely see the creeks since everyplace, apart from the houses and gardens, was underwater. Once we were out of Tawku this sheet of water covered miles of land, with clumps of grass or small trees poking up bravely from the muddy surface.

The villagers who took us knew their waterways well, and our boats turned this way and that over paddy fields now completely underwater. Once we saw a small lonely hut in the middle of nowhere, probably a family staying near their gaggle of ducks swimming nearby. The hut was entirely made out of bright orange plastic. It would do for the duration of the monsoon but once October came, the dry weather would make it stiflingly hot.

That day we could only make it to Kyar Kike; the water was so shallow the motorized boat had to go slowly. After Ma Hlaing and

I stayed in Kyar Kike, Kyaw and a few members of our relief team climbed into light skiffs and went farther toward the sea. After we had finished giving out plastic pails, we overheard recipients saying to each other, "Mine is red! It's prettier than your blue!" "I like green; may I change my red one for yours?"

By late afternoon our work was done and we sat in our boat waiting for Kyaw and the others to return. Our boatman did not know the way back, so we could not return to our truck but had to wait for Kyaw's boatman, who was a local. As we waited and talked over the things we still needed to do, Kyar Kike villagers kept coming one by one to plead with us to come and eat dinner at their house. We hadn't the heart to eat any of their food so shared a bag of biscuits and a bunch of bananas. We accepted the hot green tea that people brought when they saw some of us shivering in damp clothes in the stiff breeze.

As we waited we watched the villagers take their evening baths. The adults bathed decorously, but the children frolicked like seals. While we watched the cavorting water babies, we saw a couple of men rowing to shore in half a skiff. The front half had been destroyed by the cyclone, so when they needed to use it they had to sit well back in the stern. They were then able to lift the front out of the water, which prevented the boat from sinking and kept them mobile. They told us they had just come back from Tawku.

We saw a dog with a dead duck in its jaws trotting proudly along a narrow path and turn toward a hut. I had seen dogs ... what few survived ... at times trying, unsuccessfully I might add, to catch swimming ducks by suddenly belly-flopping into the water. This one apparently had more skill and was going home to host a duck dinner for his human family.

The pale sun vanished below the horizon of flooded paddy fields that looked like an ocean. The sunset was not gold and pink; it was steely silver, somber, the color of despair. In the darkening sky the stars began to appear. There was a wispy layer of cloud like a chiffon scarf all over the sky so the stars were not shining brightly. First we saw hundreds, then thousands of hazy points of light. We could see rather well by their soft glow although there was no moon.

Kyaw arrived at last, and we called out in delight when we saw the light of his torch from the prow of his boat; by then we were aching all over, although our wet clothes had dried on our bodies. Kyaw told us the village he went to was so far away, he could only unload, report to the abbot, and leave immediately. If he had spent more time there, we would have been waiting until dawn. It was very late by the time we were back at Kunchangon Monastery, but the abbot, other monks, and the helper ladies were still up, waiting for us with a hot meal.

On July 4 I again went with Kyaw and Ma Hlaing by boat to six villages, among them Banbwe Ngu and Paya Lay Ngu, to donate mosquito nets, rice, noodle packets, and other goods. By that time new leaves covered the scarred trees so the look of devastation was, on the surface, gone.

We had to walk for about thirty minutes from the boat landing to Paya Lay Ngu on narrow, muddy dikes. On each side the paddy fields were flooded. I knew, from what the locals had told me, that leeches the size of baby carrots swim in them or nestle in the tufts of grass on the dikes to jump on succulent feet and then cling like ... well, leeches. I was walking barefoot as my plastic slippers were extremely slippery in the mud, and I was sure that a leech would easily spot my bare soles. Luckily none feasted on me and I only saw one fat one writhing in ecstasy on the ground, apparently already well fed. A tremor of terror and queasiness shivered through my nerves.

The villagers were gathered at the monastery as prearranged by "our" abbot. Kyaw and the two young monks who came with us went off in three different directions, Kyaw by boat and the other two on foot, each accompanied by a few villagers and one or two of our team carrying bags of rice and other things for more remote villages.

When they came back in the evening, one of our team members, Sarbo, said that in one village there was a three-year-old girl living with her sixty-five-year-old grandmother; the rest of her family had died in the storm. Sarbo, who is a mechanic with a large family to support, was in despair that he could not afford to adopt the child.

"The old lady's so feeble! How will they live! How can she look after her properly!" He worried all the way home.

We had hoped to give every household in one village a mosquito net, but after we arrived in Kunchangon our abbot sent us to another group of villages that urgently needed help, so we decided to hold a mosquito net lottery for each of the six villages we went to that day. At Paya Lay Ngu the abbot had prepared lunch for us and insisted that we eat when we arrived at 3 p.m. By then we had eaten from the lunch boxes we brought with us, so only Ma Hlaing and I managed to swallow a few polite mouthfuls so that nobody would have hurt feelings.

The ladies there had prepared chicken curry, fresh greens to dip in a relish, a savory omelette filled with spring onions, and a soup of gwe tauk leaves in chicken broth. The leaves, which are slightly bitter but medicinal, were freshly picked from the vine, dipped into boiling broth, and then served immediately, making the best soup we had in years. Chicken is the favored curry to serve guests, as some do not eat beef, or pork, or avoid all red meat; so it is the fate of village chickens to face life-threatening situations when guests are expected or arrive unexpectedly. Villagers know that their neighbor has a guest just by hearing the sound of shrieking chickens. They will send a dish or two of what they have in their pots over to that house, to make the neighbor's meal abundant. When they have guests other households will do the same, to help each other demonstrate the good hospitality offered by the village. "Rallying around" is an integral feature of rural communities.

Another rural attribute is to show appreciation for help. Ma Hlaing told me that once after they handed out supplies, their truck was leaving a village and was gaining speed when a girl ran after it to dump a bag on Ma Hlaing's lap, calling "Present! Present!" It was a dozen very tiny eggs from what were probably badly traumatised ducks. The "victims" of the storm were always so grateful to those who brought donations that they would insist on feeding their visitors or giving to them. Donors had to refuse emphatically or run away as fast as they could.

The lottery of mosquito nets at each village was a great success. Ma Hlaing had bought two sizes, one 7 feet by 7 feet for the whole family, and a smaller number of single nets for old people. We kept back the singles, rather than have the old folks try their luck, and gave them away to any elderly person whom we met.

The singles were in white while the family ones were in extremely bright tones of pink, mauve, blue, and green. Those who did not pick a lucky ticket laughed at their bad luck and those who did beamed happily. Some said the nets were bigger than their huts and it was a great joke that the huts could be inside the net instead of the other way around. As usual there was a "changing of the colors."

I went to the delta when I had things to donate purchased with funds given by my friends, but Ma Hlaing and her family went over sixty times. When they went, Kyaw kept a record of useful data on the villages he visited or of others he had not gone to yet whose representatives came to see him at the Kunchangon monastery—which happened every time they went. If he could find funds to help them he would but if not, he would pass the data on to other relief groups.

By early August, things were beginning to wind down. Ma Hlaing and Kyaw could no longer go as often or give as much.

However, July 17 was the most important religious day in Myanmar, the Full Moon of Waso, and they wanted to give the community surrounding our Kunchangon monastery a Sadu Ditha, or a free meal. In less trying times this would be a normal feast to have in rural communities all over the country. Ma Hlaing and Kyaw thought it would give this community a chance to recapture something from their former lives in the aftermath of the tragedy—plus it would give a boost to their spirits and ours.

Our abbot would give a sermon and we would share our merit gained from the feast with all guests, as well as with those who had lost their lives in the storm. Kyaw had spent nights at far-flung villages and he and the team members told us that in the dead of night they had heard sounds of people scrabbling desperately to get on the roof. No one was there when they got up to look, and none of them could go back to sleep afterward.

It is a Buddhist belief that those who die violent deaths are not aware of their fate for some time, and think they are still in the last terrifying moments of their lives. Sharing merit like this enables them to realize that they must move on to their next existence and be reborn ... depending upon the sort of person they had been, to a better or lower life: celestial, human, or cockroach and variants in between. (If born human, they would be rich or not, lucky or not, depending upon how they had behaved in their former lives.)

Excitedly we made plans for the feast. Our abbot called from Kunchangon saying that he expected five thousand people to attend, with four hundred monks and nuns from all the monasteries of Kunchangon arriving at 4 a.m. on their morning alms-rounds. Five thousand! And four hundred!

More excitement, more planning, and more shopping, and on the afternoon of the sixteenth we were on our way. I brought along

a dozen new knives for the peeling and cutting I thought we could help with—fat chance. The ladies of the community shooed us away from the dozens of women who sat around the low tables, peeling and cutting mountainous piles of onions, potatoes, pumpkins, beans, eggplants, and radishes.

Others were in the kitchen frying the onion slices. Onion oil and crisp, golden onion slices are essential ingredients in our cuisine, especially for the shrimp paste relish they were preparing. To get the onion slices out of the bubbling hot oil in the nick of time before they turn dark and bitter takes precision and attention.

As they had to fry mountains of onion slices in woks like wash-tubs, I wondered how they would manage to scoop up the frying slices before they burned. Then I saw their contraption, a bamboo basket woven like a sieve with a very long upright handle. They placed the onion slices in the basket and then they dipped the whole basket into the oil. They stirred the onion slices a few times and at the right moment, simply lifted the basket out of the oil in one move. Bravo.

We had a great dinner at the monastery as usual, with our favorite dish, hin baung: "Mixture Dish." Monks on their morning alms-rounds return with servings of different curries, vegetables, or soup given by people all over town. After their meal, anything left over, except for the rice, is put into a huge pot and cooked together with some tart roselle leaves and a few green chillies. This "collection" stew is served to monks with rice for breakfast the next day or to visitors for dinner. It sounds horrible described like this, but it is one of the best dishes I know and you can't copy it at home. Maybe it's the perfect hand of the monastery volunteers or the slow simmering, but it's so good. Every time we ate at the monastery, this is the dish we demanded and were given, a huge bowl in the middle of the table with many spoons stuck in it. There were fried velvet beans, crisp on the outside and soft inside. There were other curries made with pork or fish, but the hin baung and beans disappeared quickest into our deep gullets.

Around 2 a.m., the ladies were still cooking. The vegetable stew was simmering in immense pots that looked big enough to cook two whole pigs at once. Rice was being cooked in stacks of trays inside a huge cylindrical steamer like a spaceship, which they lowered onto or lifted off the fire by means of a pulley and rope. The community seemed easily capable of cooking for five thousand; after all, this is one of their customary feasts.

At 4 a.m. the monks of the town began to arrive, and heading them were the monks from our monastery, led by our abbot! We had planned to serve him breakfast, along with his community of monks, in the comfort of the dining room, but to honor us he had chosen to walk in line with his alms bowl. His junior monks, by now as close to us as family, kept their faces solemn and dignified as they filed past us with lowered eyes. For this alms-round ritual, we offered pork curry ("chunks like fists," as we say in Burmese) as well as vegetable stew, relish, and slices of raw cucumber that was to be the menu for our guests.

There were nuns, too, led by their abbesses. I was delighted to see them. Usually they do not go on morning alms-rounds but do so during the whole pre-fast day, collecting dry goods and cash from donors.

By 7:30 a.m. our first guests had arrived and ear-splitting religious songs began to play, transmitted through horn-shaped loudspeakers (or "lor," as we call them, derived from "loud"—what else?). We are a cheerful people, preferring to make jokes and have fun instead of moaning and weeping, and, especially in rural communities, music at special occasions must be played loud-loud-loud enough to declare to all for miles around that everyone's having fun.

The first screeching notes nearly felled me flat on my face but in a while my ears got used to its exuberance, and it did indeed make a difference. The loudness gave an uplifting and hopeful mood to the whole affair, even if our eardrums were under vicious attack the whole morning.

Our abbot had built temporary covered walkways just in case it rained, but the weather was balmy with cool breezes and bright with sunshine. One large ground floor hall had been turned into a dining room. Empty wooden crates used to transport duck eggs had been lined up with a yard or so between each of them, and wide planks of lumber were placed end to end over these crates. Plastic sheets covered the planks and voila! We had long tables of the right height to accommodate people who would be sitting on the ground to eat.

The hall held easily three hundred people at each seating. Children were fed in another hall, and they too ate a lot, at least two plates of rice. (One plateful for a rural person, child or man, is about double the size of an urban serving.) They all ate slowly, daintily picking up mouthfuls of rice with a bit of stew or relish with their carefully washed right hands, enjoying the simple fare. I noticed that the relish went quickly. The servers refilled the bowls as needed, carrying enameled buckets of stew or relish and plates of sliced cucumbers.

There was no chaos; people came, ate, talked to friends, and left, and their places were taken by another batch. One group washed dishes; others carried trays of food, or removed the empty plates. One group refilled the buckets of water set out so that people could wash hands before and after eating. Some discreetly swept the sand on the polished wooden floor around people's legs, sand carried in by bare feet. There were mats to wipe feet at the entrances but they were not enough.

When we sat down to our lunch after almost all the guests had been served, I found out why they had eaten with so much enjoyment. I never liked pumpkin before but that stew, with pumpkins almost melting away in the gravy, was unbelievably delicious. The relish was the right ratio of saltiness, hotness, and tartness. The balance of stew and relish was made perfect by the crisp, sweet cucumbers. It was one of the best meals I have ever eaten in my life.

Other welfare groups that were also based in "our" monastery dropped in and they too were invited to have lunch. They liked the food so much that they begged us for some relish to take home to Yangon.

Afterward we listened to our abbot give a sermon on the upper story of the building where we fed the guests. His disciples packed the hall to overflowing, sitting tightly against each other. Tears welled up in our eyes as he intoned the words of sharing the merit with all who had died tragically.

I hoped, we all hoped, that the dead-but-unaware were with us that day listening to his sermon, and that, strengthened by his words, they would find peace at last and be reborn into a better life, a safer life.

CHAPTER TWELVE

Hitching a Ride to the Second Century

Several months after making trips to the delta, I was aboard a beautiful little teak boat used for tourism, hitching a ride to Pyay from Yangon on the RV Pandaw. Pyay is very near the ancient ruined city of Srikhetera, where the Pyu civilization flourished from the second to the eighth centuries.

Pyay is an ancient name which the British turned into Prome. The story goes that when the first British officer stepped ashore he came upon an old man putting finishing touches to a basket he was weaving.

"What is this town?" he demanded in English.

"Town" (Taung) being the word in Burmese for an open, wide-topped basket, the old man had spat out in Burmese: "It's a p'lone, you idiot, can't you see it's a p'lone!" (A p'lone is a covered basket with a narrow opening and a strap.)

All Asians mix up their r's and l's—after all, the Chinese do that, don't they?—thus the British accepted the name as Prome, so the joke went, with the city of Pyay renamed after a basket.

To travel that part of the river between Yangon and the prosperous and deeply Buddhist town of Pyay was a challenge I could not meet for two years. As it takes a mere six hours by car, few travel that stretch of the river by boat anymore. Luckily for me Andrea Massari, a nice Italian guy working for a travel agency, mentioned to me that his Pandaw had been in the Yangon dry docks since May for post-Nargis repairs and would leave at the end of August to pick up a large group of tourists at Bagan.

He was happy to offer me a ride on it, but told me apologetically that there would be some carpenters on board to apply finishing touches of lacquer and polish to furniture and the wooden floors. I assured him I'd be happy to be part of the crew, and that I could be helpful perhaps, since I was pretty handy with a paintbrush considering my thirty-year career as an artist. But he insisted that I was an honored guest so I was feeling ah nar dei, or deeply obligated, even before I set foot on board.

I really wanted to be "one of the guys." Fat chance—I was to discover from day one that my age, old enough to be the mother of most of the crew, meant that I was treated with great respect. I had no chance to sandpaper floors when pitted against the politeness of two dozen young men.

I was so excited about finally doing this lap of the Ayeyarwaddy that I was packed and ready a week before the departure date. When that lovely Sunday morning rolled around I called Ko Nyi Nyi from the Pandaw Company at 6 a.m. to inform him of my imminent arrival on board. Groggy from being awakened at that ungodly hour, the poor man finally understood what I was saying and told me that it was still Saturday. It took him some minutes to convince me that I was a day early, for I kept asking him, "Are you sure, are you absolutely sure?"

I made it well in time the next morning; I had been up since four.

The Pandaw is a splendid little three-decker ship, with beautiful teak-walled cabins and teak floors. The top deck is open, very breezy, with cane chairs to lounge in and watch sunsets. I walked around barefoot, enjoying the feeling of smooth teak under my soles.

There had been a long relaunching party the previous night so the crew had been told to sleep late and report later. Monks conducted a blessing ceremony on board at nine o'clock, after which we began our journey. In minutes we were off, along the Yangon River and then down the twenty-two-mile-long Twanté Canal. As we left, many of the crew, up-country men stuck in Yangon all summer, were dancing with joy, singing, "We're going home! We're going home!" Their friends on other boats waved at them, looking envious.

An hour into the canal, I climbed onto the upper deck and saw the Yangon high-rises fade into the blue-white mist, with the Shwedagon in pale but shimmering glory looming over the skyline. Even when standing right on its platform, looking up at the 326-foot spire, you do not get the same sense of its immense size as you do from the river.

I gazed and gazed, marveling at the devotion and what seems like the sheer folly of the populace, who have adorned the spire since the fifteenth century with an estimated three tons of gold or more. The tradition continues—as I write this, the spire is being wrapped in bamboo scaffolding, as it is every decade, so new gold plates can be attached. It's a pointy Fort Knox growing skyward, visible from miles around.

I had brought as many thick novels as I could carry, the sort of silly but well-written dramatic romances that ease the mind and soothe the nerves. Out of their total of 4,162 pages, by journey's end, in less than a week, I would have read 3,149.

There was a comfortable cane chair on the deck in front of my room, and I sat for hours gazing at the passing delta. The banks of the river were choked with shrubs, trees, and reeds, but not with the tall jungles I'd seen up north. The vegetation was so thick that vines seemed ready to swallow the bamboo huts. Some of these dwellings were newly repaired, but still ramshackle; some had walls or roofs made from the plastic that had been donated to storm victims.

Sunsets on the river were spectacular, especially since we were not yet out of the monsoon season. There were enough clouds in the sky to provide a canvas for the sun's palette of scarlet, gold, mauve, and vermillion. At one turn of the river on our first day out, the water was as smooth as a mirror, placid and silken, as it reflected the brilliant evening colors.

The days went by lazily and peacefully. My meals were fabulous ... each day a different menu of delicious roast chicken, grilled chops and fries, lobster bisque, pasta in rich sauces, delicate noodles with seafood and mushrooms ... served to me in lone grandeur in the dining room. Unable to make the waiter sit at my table without clobbering him and dragging him over, I chatted while I ate as he, poor man, stood by my table.

The first waiter to serve me was Zin Lin Maung, who grew up in Bagan.

"Actually," he said, "the other side of Bagan on the sand-bank that is now an island, across the river from the Lawka Nanda Pagoda. My parents grow onions."

Out of his salary he had bought three large compounds and a house for his parents. His two younger siblings were still in school and the two extra plots were for them when they grew up. Zin Lin was justly proud of being a good son and eldest brother. He tried to get his parents to visit Yangon but his mother even hated to go to Bagan. "She says it's too crowded!"

Bagan is an utterly tranquil place with miles of empty land dotted with old temples, but many rural people react to it in the same way as Zin Lin's mother—for them, a crowd of more than twenty people is too much.

At one point I commented upon how quickly young children of Bagan pick up foreign languages.

"When I was young," he said, "during the '80s in Bagan there was this man U Taing Kyaw [meaning "Known All Over the Country"] who came here to live from somewhere else. He knew English and French very well and also some Italian, Spanish, and German. He drank a lot but not when he was teaching these lan-guages to young people—for free, you know. He would practically drag students to his class and he'd get mad if someone didn't want to learn. A lot of his students became licensed guides. He died around 1998. I think he was about fifty years old then, not older than that. We don't even know if U Taing Kyaw was his real name, but he was known as the Wild Man of Bagan."

Zin Lin had missed out on these free classes because he had been more focused on getting through high school with good marks. He now had a bachelor's degree in economics by correspondence course from the University of Yangon, but he still wished he had studied with U Taing Kyaw.

Another waiter who alternated with Zin Lin was Soe Moe Aung

from Yangon; he once worked at the lovely Monsoon Restaurant and remembered seeing me there. He was the bartender on board, and we talked about cocktails. I told him about the time when I was thirteen and one evening when Mother was out somewhere, Father decided I was old enough to learn to drink. He mixed me a martini but since I didn't like the taste, to his fury I stirred in some honey.

Some afternoons U Tun Naing, the general manager on board, talked to me while his carpenters polished the floors and hummed songs of homesickness. He was from Mandalay and a bond was instantly established when I told him my mother was a Mandalay girl and I consider it my ancestral home. He once worked at the five-star Novotel Hotel in Mandalay and when he first transferred to the Pandaw, he knew nothing of life on the water.

"I didn't know port from starboard, I didn't know anything about engines, not even the names of parts, but I carried a notebook, poked around everywhere, looked and listened all the time and wrote down everything," he said. He had been working on board for over two years and now he loved the life.

When Nargis hit, for the first two days he could not cross the Yangon River to check on the Pandaw as it lay in the dry docks of Dallah, and there was no communication. Both days he had come to sit on the Yangon bank from morning until dusk to look across to Dallah, worried sick about his boat, feeling weepy, and unable to eat anything. His wife had accused him of never yearning for her like that, but he had replied that she had never been "wounded" like his ship. When he could finally cross to Dallah, he was heartbroken to see his lovely vessel "hurt," he said. The company decided to make a thorough repair and renovation job and for this he was grateful; for him and the crew, the Pandaw had become a lovely lady whom they must tenderly look after.

Captain U Win Swe, whom I bothered a few times with questions about the river, almost burst with pride for his ship. He had been a river man for thirty-two years, ever since he was twenty-one. He talked about the Ayeyarwaddy as if it were a person, his face blazing with love when we discussed the awesome beauty of the defiles up north. He nearly took me to his bosom like a long-lost sister when he learned I'd traveled almost all along "our" river right from the confluence.

His wife lives in Mandalay and he said he always tells her to keep the household shrine fresh with flowers, water, and food.

"I told her my work is always threatened by the Five Enemies (Water, Fire, King, Thief, and One Who Does Not Love You), and a river is not someone you can plead with or scold or threaten. Rivers have their own minds."

This he said with affectionate pride as if speaking of a pretty and willful daughter.

The morning before we reached Pyay, I was writing in my cabin and dropped my pen. Stupidly I tried to pick it up without bending my knees and crack went my back. I painfully straightened myself but once upright could no longer bend at the waist. For the second time in my life I was shuffling along like a plank of wood with feet, pain shooting up my lower back when I tried to move faster.

Panic began to flap around blindly in my chest, while my mind was screaming What shall I do what shall I do, as I saw myself crawling on all fours around the boat and around the ancient temples of Srikhetera. My blood pressure rose and blood pounded in my head.

Luckily I recalled what a young computer geek once told me about the best way to calm down. I gingerly placed myself flat on the floor, emptied my thoughts, and softened my breathing until I entered what he called hibernation mode, "like that of a computer," as he had explained, barely functioning in both body and mind. Within a minute I was at peace.

The first time my back went out of whack, I was lucky to have the phone number of U Zaw Linn Htet, an "accupressurist," as he liked to be called. He thought a chiropractor only dealt with problems of the feet and he disliked the name. His mother was a renowned indigenous healer, honored with a medal by U Nu, the prime minister of our democratic period after independence. A year before I hurt my back, I had heard of her son's prowess and had noted down his number "just in case." So on that morning six years ago, when in somewhat the same circumstances my back suddenly gave out, I was able to call a friend to fetch him.

He had cured me in less than three minutes by having me lie on my back while he twiddled with my ankles and shook my legs to loosen them up, after which he told me to lock my knees. Then he turned each ankle outward, slowly but firmly. After making a few more turns he told me to get up, and I could, easily, while before I could hardly lift my head. There was still some pain, which he rubbed away with an ointment and that was that.

What I now suffered alone in my cabin was not as bad as that first time, so still lying on the floor and inwardly praying hard, I shook my legs slightly, locked my knees and turned my ankles outward. Doing this the whole morning and rubbing Tiger Balm on my back cured me by lunchtime.

The next morning we were at Pyay. I said thank you and goodbye to the boys, and was carefully helped along three connecting gangplanks by a member of the crew. I waved back at them, hailed a trishaw, and soon was at my Pyay oasis, the Mingalar Garden Hotel. I would be staying only one night, I said, and could they find me a car to take me to the old city right now?

The car came half an hour later. I told the driver to go first to the bus depot to get me a ticket to Yangon the next day; if we were in time I would be able to get a seat on the earliest bus. The driver turned in his seat to look at me; I stared back stupidly, my mind going What!? What!??

He finally and apologetically said that he was going down to Yangon himself early the next day to drive his son to an interview, and for a small fee I could come with him and he'd drive me home. I gave a few delighted bounces on my seat; I was pleased that I need not bother about a taxi ride from the bus depot in Yangon, miles in the outskirts, to my downtown flat. Yes, yes, yes, I'd be happy to.

"We leave at five," he warned. No problem for me.

With no need for a bus ticket, I told him to go straight to the Pyu pagodas and the small museum nearby. There, what interested me most were the huge stone funeral urns, their bottoms incised with Pyu letters. The calligraphy is utterly beautiful, with elegant swirls and graceful, swooping lines.

The Pyu had been a gentle race, so deeply Buddhist that they would not wear silk as it "involves injury to life" of the worms.

We have few written records left of them in Myanmar, but Chinese texts—the Man-shu and the New T'ang histories—give details about their civilization, most notably the Man-shu, written by Fan Ch'o around 864 CE, thirty-two years after the Pyu kingdom was destroyed by forces from Nan Ch'ao. Thousands had been taken prisoner, and the remnants of this rich civilization had resettled farther north where two centuries later they were assimilated into the flourishing civilization of Bagan.

It was the custom of the Pyu "to love life and hate killing," the Chinese wrote. They had no "chains or fetters" but punished criminals by beating them with stalks of bamboo, and for murder, death.

The Chinese noted that the Pyu king's palace in Srikhetera and the "over one hundred" Buddhist monasteries there were "decked out with gold and silver, coated with cinnabar and bright colors, smeared with kino [red-colored tree sap] and covered with embroidered rugs." When the king went on a short journey, "he is borne

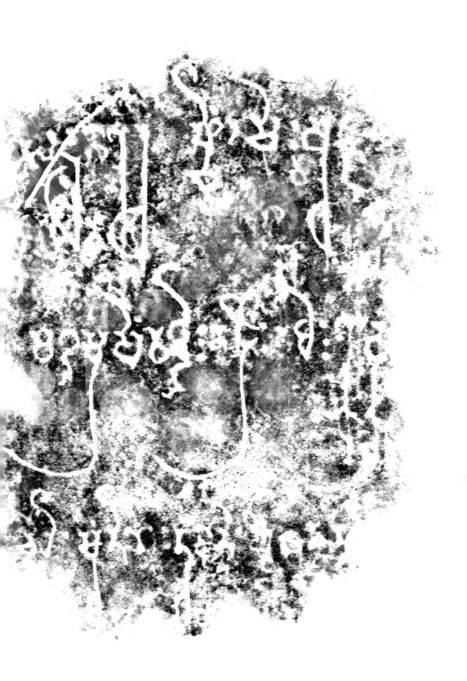

in a litter of golden cord. When the journey is far, he rides on an elephant."

Ladies wore blue skirts of fine cotton with gauze scarves and they held fans. Their hair was ornamented with strings of pearls and piled in coils on top of their heads. The men wore gold-flowered hats and caps of kingfisher feathers strung with jewels. They greeted each other by grasping an arm with a hand while lowering their heads as a sign of respect. They were "acquainted with astronomy and delighted in Buddha's Law."

The fields in this region have yielded gold artifacts, ornaments, silver coins, and beads to plowing farmers. The National Museum in Yangon once held a Pyu exhibition and people lined up for hours to see the delicate and exquisite jewelry, some pieces so intricate and tiny that modern goldsmiths declared they had no idea how to copy them. There were beads of gold in all sizes and so modern in design that they could have been made for shops in Paris; minute agate seals with delicately carved indentations of birds, animals, and figures, once set in rings and used as seals; four-inch-long beads with narrow bores that would only take an ultrafine thread and had a sort of bendy turn in the middle. Yangon artisans scratched their heads and found no answer to the tools the ancients had used.

Terrence Tan, a young scholar who admits that he is obsessed with Pyu artifacts, has often shown me items from his collection of Pyu jewelry. Among them was something that to me symbolizes the epitome of the Pyu civilization: a small bronze ball that produced musical sounds when moved. When a damaged one was cut in half to see how it worked, it revealed three layers of bronze set slightly apart within a shell, the better to give resonance to the tune. Each layer was made of intersecting triangular chips. When shaken, a small bronze pellet trapped inside ran along the ridges formed by these chips to make different notes. It was an intricate and playful thing, created solely for the sake of pleasure.

Now, centuries after this art had flourished, I walked around the base of the high cylindrical shape of the Baw Baw Pagoda in the midst of empty wild meadows dotted with thick shrubs and leafy trees. There was not a single soul in sight apart from my driver and me. In the afternoon heat, birds slumbered and made no song.

I envisioned the Pyu of nearly twelve hundred years ago, the elegant ladies and lordly gentlemen walking the busy streets of their city, escorted by their servants. They would come to the Baw Baw Pagoda, I thought. They would bring flowers and pray. They would visit golden monasteries and at times step aside to make way for the king and retinue. How their gold, kingfisher feathers, and jewels would flash in the sun!

And perhaps, a bronze ball would be shaken in the idle fingers of a lady on a lazy afternoon and its music would celebrate their civilization.

CHAPTER THIRTEEN

Great Balloons of Fire

It was already dark, at 6 p.m.

A tight circle of men squatted on the ground, their fingers clutching the rim of a hole in the bottom of a fire balloon (or hot-air balloon) that loomed thirty feet over their heads. The top of the balloon had first been lifted up with a hook on a long bamboo pole held by a man who stood precariously on top of a shaky eight-foot-high stand of hammered planks and bamboo. Once the smoke began to fill the balloon, the hook was removed and now the balloon slowly stretched skyward. The smoke rising from the torches held under the opening slowly expanded the balloon, which in a few minutes would be struggling to break free and rise to the pagoda in the heavens.

It was the night before the Full Moon Day of Tazaung Daing or November, the month of the most marvelous moon and the most beautiful stars. It is an old tradition to set off fire balloons at night, to honor the Sulamuni Pagoda in the sky built by the King of the Celestials and enshrining the Buddha's hair. No matter that no earthly being has seen it; Buddhists know it is there.

Ma Hlaing, Kyaw, their boys, and I were again at the Kunchangon monastery, months after our Nargis relief expeditions. Our abbot stood on the balcony, looking on with a pleased smile. Hundreds of villagers stood in a circle a safe distance from the balloon, while younger men and children danced wildly to the thumping beats of a country song remixed with hip-hop, blaring from huge amplifiers loud enough to pierce our ears.

Since we were on holy monastic grounds, everyone was barefoot. I skipped around the squatting men holding onto the balloon while I tried to get good shots with my small camera, at times jumping with yelps of pain when my bare soles met cinders scattered on the ground. Kyaw shot a few scenes and then went to join the men who held onto the balloon.

Two new events had cropped up during the past ten years or so—the fire balloon competitions in Taungyi and Pyin Oo Lwin—but here in the monastery, the balloon launch was something that the present abbot ... and all previous ones ... had spent decades arranging for the community to enjoy. A note signed by the abbot is always sent up with the balloons, and whoever finds it wins a sum of thirty thousand kyat or more.

The balloons, made of cloth or paper, are fueled with smoke from burning rags. The rags are soaked in a tin of petroleum and are kept in place under the balloons' openings with strong rigging.

Men or women in the community who can make the balloons are highly sought after each year. At other times they have different jobs, but come November they are kept busy in their "real" profession. The costs are funded by the abbot and the community; many might be in dire straits after the cyclone, but no one was about to give up the traditions that they have upheld for as long as they can remember. I doubt if even the bombing of World War II managed to stop the people of Myanmar from holding their annual festivals.

That afternoon I had watched people inside a large hall as they put finishing touches on three balloons, one made of thick green paper, another of red, and the last, the biggest at forty feet, of handmade paper. The first two were in fine condition, but the biggest, made of squares of thin mulberry paper that in places looked as fragile as old white lace, needed some patching. Two electric fans whirled into the opening and inflated the balloon while men and monks walked in dizzying circles around it, checking for leaks. Backlit with sunlight that poured through the windows, the balloon slowly filled out like a mammoth translucent cocoon.

As the night darkened and the balloon grew bigger, the flame at its bottom turned it into a fat, red bulb that fingers could no longer grip; and the squatting men stood up slowly, their arms held high, and, in unison, let go. Accompanied by shouts of jubilation

from adults and shrieks of delight from children, it rose majestically but with incredible speed, and within a few seconds it was only a small bob of light. The dancing grew wilder, children raced about in excitement, and the laboring men wiped floods of sweat from their

brows. We craned our necks to keep it in sight until its light mingled with the stars, relieved that it did not burst into flame on its ascent.

Monasteries in other neighborhoods also sent up their balloons during this three-day period of the full moon, and for weeks afterward the whole town buzzed with gossip as to whose balloons had lasted the longest. The event is a ritual not only of enjoyment but of prestige as well, and we were proud that all of our balloons went up successfully.

Every village and almost every monastery in the country sends off fire balloons. Shops now sell cheap kiddie-sized plastic balloons in a multitude of colors that can be inflated by using a candle, so if people are watching from space at this time of year, they will see the dark sky over Myanmar filled with bobbing lights.

We ate dinner prepared in abundance by the ladies who help out at the monastery, the same ones who had cooked all night for our free feast in July. For a while after we sat down around the low round tables, all that could be seen were flashing spoons and hands reaching for the hin baung bowl that contained our favorite stew.

After we were reasonably full, we crunched our way through piles of boiled crabs while the monastery cats mewed and butted their heads against our knees. The dining room was also the sleeping quarters of some younger monks and novices and they, who had not eaten since noon, sat and read or chatted a few feet away from us, quite undistracted by our gluttony.

After dinner, before we all went to bed in another large hall lined up in our mosquito nets, men on one side and women on the other, I chanced to mention to a local man that I would like to take a ride on a bamboo raft; could he help me?

He, a devotee of our abbot and one of Ma Hlaing's good friends, said bamboo rafts stop at Kunchangon on their way southward, and he promised to check it out for me. Suddenly I spotted Ma Hlaing giving him a look that said, "Not going to happen."

I realized instantly that he would not dare arrange something for me that she considered dangerous, and that would probably also be discouraged by our abbot.

Ma Hlaing is one of the kindest people I know, her soft heart hidden by her feisty manner and lively tongue. Younger than I by about fifteen years, she worries about my welfare more than my mother ever did. It was the biggest mistake I ever made to mention a raft in her presence.

I had forgotten my rule never to allow friends or family to know what I was up to until it's all done, as I had learned when I was a toddler trying to fool Mother. There would be hailstorms in hell before I got to set foot on one of these rafts, since Ma Hlaing's friend was the only person I had found who had admitted he could help me. Happily bloated with hin baung and sweet crabmeat, I had been lulled into carelessness.

The next day, I would go to Pyapon in a taxi and return to Yangon by boat. I wanted to write an article about an annual event in Pyapon that began some 130 years ago, a folk theater performance of the Ramayana that lasts nine days. It usually takes place around the October full moon, but the cyclone had destroyed the Pyapon theater so the event was postponed by a month.

Ma Hlaing and her family were on their way home to Yangon early the next morning, while I waited for a taxi to pick me up. I had invited anyone who might want a ride to Pyapon to come along, and a monk with his layman assistant accompanied me.

Some days before our trip I had asked Ma Hlaing to book me a room in a Pyapon hotel owned by one of her friends. When I arrived, the manager there told me there was no room reserved for me nor any vacant rooms at all, and sent me to another hotel. It was bigger and flashier with horrifying, bright blue mirrored glass all over the front. The monk, his assistant, and the taxi driver had all gone in with me to the front desk, showing that, although I might seem to be a woman alone, I was not without protection, only to learn that this place was full as well.

Finally we arrived at one inn right by the docks, a fleabag place that fortunately turned out to have no fleas. My companions stuck with me long enough to make sure I was good and settled and, after looking over the few men lolling in tattered cane chairs in the "lobby," loudly told me before they departed to call them at once should I need anything—not that I knew their numbers or if they even had phones.

Since I was going home by boat, I thought it was actually better that I was so near the docks. From the top of the stairs going up to my room I could see the river and the triple-decker boat that I would take, which sparkled with fresh white and blue paint.

In contrast to my boat, the walls, ceiling, and floor of my room on the second floor were grimy, as far as I could see from the faint light from one window. That opening was screened with dusty mosquito-proof netting and faced a brick wall of the neighboring

building just inches away. At least no one could peep into the room, I thought.

There was no blanket on the bed, just a thin, hard mattress covered with a washed but discolored bedsheet printed with unhappy-looking teddy bears. The pillow was hard and in a shabby but clean case. There was a fan and a bare light bulb on the wall at the foot of my bed, so reading in bed was out. Dangling wires and a loose socket did not look too safe but I hoped they would have enough power to recharge my camera battery. That I could not do right away because there was no electricity until evening, I found out after trudging all the way down to the front desk.

I unpacked, washed up, and went out to the bustling market next to the hotel to forage for breakfast. I had monhinga, the fish-broth noodles that Pyapon is famous for, and although the shop was just a rickety wooden table and a few stools, the noodle dish was good. Afterward I strolled along the pavement where shops

sold vegetables and fish. There were cucumbers like logs, a size I never see in Yangon. City people do not like big cucumbers, the vegetable seller told me when I mentioned it, but here they cook the cucumbers in a stew—which Yangonites never do.

"You cook it just like winter melon," she assured me, telling me the recipe: "Peel it, remove the seeds, and cut into cubes. Stew with a tiny bit of oil, fish sauce, and dried prawns. It's delicious." I promised to try.

A row of phones sat outside a tea shop. After making a call to Ma Hlaing, who by then was back in Yangon, to tell her of my whereabouts, I went back to my room and tried to nap.

I was not to rest long. Apparently Ma Hlaing had called her Pyapon contacts, found out what happened, and given them hell, all of which I learned when a young woman, a total stranger, knocked on my door. She looked both upset and embarrassed, and I was wondering if my taxi had almost run over her or something like that, until she explained everything.

She knew both Ma Hlaing and the hotel owner, and had heard through the grapevine before I arrived that a woman alone would be putting up at a hotel. She was worried, I think, that I would be prey to strange men who would perhaps think my behavior scandalous, if not "easy," since it was rare that a Myanmar woman would travel on her own. Thus out of the kindness of her heart she had decided it would be more appropriate for me to stay at her house and had told the hotel owner not to reserve a room for me.

To offer free bed and board to a stranger is not at all out of the way for a Myanmar family, and it was truly thoughtful and kind of her to be so protective of another woman's decency. But I needed, and preferred, to be alone—to relax as I wanted, sprawled on my bed at all hours, and to work on my notes at any time of day or night, without having polite conversations with my hostess and her family.

My visitor was dismayed by the condition of my room and with profuse, almost teary apologies, insisted that I move to her home at once. I assured her repeatedly that because I would be going back by boat this was the best place to be, both to buy a ticket and to get on board, especially since my boat would leave at night to arrive in Yangon quite early the next morning.

She finally asked if she might accompany me to the show, and I knew it was because she felt it was inhospitable to allow a friend of a friend to go out alone in the evening. This too I refused firmly, for I would not be the type of audience she was used to, someone who sits in front of the stage nibbling melon seeds and sipping green tea. She would be most uncomfortable hanging around backstage with me. She left only half-convinced, and after her departure my cheeks ached from all of the smiling I'd done during her visit.

I went back to bed, but was roused two hours later when a maid knocked on my door to tell me I had more visitors downstairs. They turned out to be the owner and the manager of the hotel I'd first gone to, and they offered profuse apologies for not having a room for me. I reassured them many times over that it was not their fault, my room here was perfect, and so was the location, since it was just a step away from the boat.

After these visitors departed, I tottered back to bed. That night would be the first of the Ramayana performances that would take place over the next nine days, and I would be backstage until the show ended at dawn. I had no idea how many nights I would need to stay in order to interview the entire cast.

CHAPTER FOURTEEN

Meeting a Lovely Ogress

Princess Gambi, the sister of Prince Rama's archenemy, the ogre King Datha Giri, is my favorite character in the Ramayana. Complex and strong, she is a villain with ice-cold anger and passionate vengeance in her evil heart. I've always thought she was more interesting than Princess Sita, who sent first her husband Prince Rama and then her brother-in-law Lekhana into certain danger, all because she wanted a pretty deer, an ogre in disguise, as a pet. Besides, Sita embodies Virtue, which I have no inclination whatsoever to possess.

(One of my great-grandmothers was a Thai lady descended from a family brought over from Ayutthaya in the eighteenth century, and descendants from that family line in Mandalay worship annually at a Rama shrine. It was a small wooden shed when I last saw it a decade ago, with rows of masks from the epic, but naturally without any of the ogres' faces. The masks are freshly painted every year so that by now they are thick with layers of gouache. Considering this lineage, I had no business preferring Gambi over Sita, a fact which I kept from my family.)

Pyay's Ramayana performances are free. The costs of the annual production are collected from the town, and there are many prosperous local businesspeople who usually chip in with substantial amounts. This year, however, everyone had lost something ... and many had lost everything ... so it was harder to get funds, but a few dedicated men had donated enough to build the performance hall.

All of the cast members live in the town of Pyay, except for the dancer who plays the role of Princess Sita. I intended to interview each performer for a paper I planned to write on the Ramayana tradition.

That morning, I found out later, most of the cast had gathered backstage to go through the annual ritual of offering food to the masks. For the "good" role masks, they offered rice cakes, fruits, and milk, and bananas for the monkeys. For the "evil" masks of the ogres they offered fried fish, chicken, and prawns. Actually, ogres eat raw meat but nobody was prepared to go that far, for who knew what evil spirits would be attracted by the scent of fresh blood and decide to join the play?

It was now getting dark and Ma Hlaing's friend and performer in this evening's Ramayana, U Moe Kyaw Aung, and I walked to the theater, climbing up rickety wooden steps to get backstage. There against the far wall was a table, on which were lined up the "good" masks: those of the Bodaw, Rama, Sita, Lekhana, and the monkeys.

The masks were gorgeous: the Bodaw had a dismayed expression, teeth bared. I have no idea why all the Bodaw masks I have seen are made like this. However, onstage it seemed to fit all situations, for don't wise people like the Bodaw go around looking dismayed at the foibles of humans?

The Rama mask was painted a deep emerald green with a Sita mask by its side, a bland, pretty one that Sita dancers never wear anyway. The Sita role is the only one not requiring a mask but for the purpose of being displayed as a family group, a mask for her is always present. The Lekhana mask, my favorite of all, was gold. There is no sight more stunning than Lekhana in full costume, virtually a golden god.

There were no actors there yet, as the show would begin at nine thirty (nine thirty!) and U Moe Kyaw Aung said they would only arrive an hour before. I went back to my room and fell into bed. Backstage there were usually no chairs to sit in and I could foresee hours of leg-numbing sitting on the floor or lying flat in a corner if I did not want to be on my feet all night. At quarter past eight, I tied my sweater around my waist, locked my room after me, and was back at the stage within ten minutes.

This time I cut through the pagoda, where tea and noodle shops ranged along the wide cement walkway and a large woman was already cooking batter-covered fingers of gourd and ripe plantains that bobbed in her gigantic wok of smoking oil. I entered on stage

left where two small rooms were screened off with bamboo mats. One was the dressing room of the dancer playing Sita, and in the other there were the masks of the "enemy," the ogres, on a table.

The lady playing Gambi was already sitting on the floor by the side of the table with her legs tucked under her. A large, flat, wooden box which held her costumes stood against the wall nearby. I dipped my head and lowered my shoulders as I passed to take photos of the ogre masks.

The Datha Giri head was beautiful, with shiny, curving, steel fangs instead of the normal white-painted ones. It seemed like a recent addition to the otherwise ancient-looking mask. I have seen this on other Datha Giri masks, but the steel fangs do not have the impact that the white ones do, for steel does not show up brilliantly against the green and gold scrolls of the cheeks. The spire of the ogre-king's crown was made of the special Thayo clay, a traditional mixture of fine ash from bone or wood or leaves, soft cooked rice, and a bit of lacquer sap, which is applied only to wood or lacquerware and then is completely gilded. The crown was surrounded by nine small heads and set with faux gems, as were the crowns of Rama and Lekhana and a few other ogre masks. Although they did not look 130 years old, they were well-made older models, while some of the newer ones for minor roles were made out of papier-mâché and painted with gouache.

Gambi glanced up at me, looking rather reserved, I thought. I folded my knees under me as gracefully as I could manage and sat down next to her.

I addressed her as A'ma, or "Elder Sister," and told her I had come earlier but no one was here then, and asked if she had to come a long way? Our conversation began and although she relaxed she still retained a slight reserve. It was not shyness; it was the innate dignity found often in rural Myanmar women, especially those past fifty.

Her name was Daw Nge, or "Ms. Small." She was sixty-two, tiny, and thin, her hair scraped back into a bun from a face with lovely bone structure. She had a well-formed, small nose, steady, bright black eyes, and thin but prettily curving lips. She was a professional dancer who had married a dancer. They both performed with a troupe from Bogalay, another delta town.

"Ours was also a Ramayana troupe, you know, it's not only Pyapon that has it," she said when she noticed my look of surprise. "Our Bogalay Ramayana troupe traveled and performed professionally while the Pyapon one only takes place once a year, in its own town."

Her husband had been a master dancer of the troupe, playing various parts and together they had performed the Ramayana all over the country. Nineteen years ago their troupe disbanded, possibly because by the mid-1980s younger people were beginning to lose interest in the traditional classical theater—movies on video-cassettes had arrived and every village had a video hall.

After giving up the arts, her husband decided to settle in Pyapon and Daw Nge became the Pyapon Gambi.

A tall young woman, with her flesh bulging like small pincushions all over her body, came in dragging a small boy who was the exact replica of Daw Nge. They were her youngest daughter and grandson. At the sight of the little boy, all skin and bones, Daw Nge's face lit up in a dazzling smile which made her look young and utterly charming. In that instant I could see her as a girl and how she must have stopped the hearts of men who saw this smile. People always look better when they are smiling but some have ravishing smiles that make others catch their breath. Hers was one.

When her daughter went off again, leaving her son sleeping in a corner, "Sita," the professional dancer Thwe Thwe Win or "Slender Slender Bright" from Yangon, came to pay her respects to Daw Nge. She was already in full makeup and dress, glittering with brilliants and sequins and faux diamonds in her hair and ears, around her neck and wrists, and wearing the gold headdress of a princess. She had lifted up the long train of her classical wraparound garment and had tied the ends around her to keep it clean and to prevent anyone from tripping on it and breaking his teeth. While dancing, even very quickly, the dancers are able to flick the train so that it swirls and floats behind them, which is part of the choreography.

Thwe told me that she was a graduate of the State School of Fine Arts, had danced for the National Troupe, and had won a gold medal in a national competition. As we chatted, she illustrated a point by "dancing" her arms and fingers around her head, and they moved like vines waving in the wind.

A stagestruck young novice often came to peep into "our" room, where some cast members were changing into their costumes. He stayed there all night, a silent small boy in the bright orange robes of the monastic order. He was an orphan, I learned after pulling him down to sit by me, and was looked after in a monastery. I asked if he wanted to dance one day, and he very properly did not answer my improper question, as I should not be enticing a robed one from his order; but his eyes lit up like stars. I felt a sudden stab of pity as I thought of young dreams that were often lost because trying not to starve was a difficult enough task. I was sorry I had asked—but, who knows ...

Then Daw Nge whispered to me that it was almost time for the opening sequence: a danced battle between a young ogre and a monkey. A boy I had noticed earlier hanging around backstage came into our room. He had spiky short hair, and some leather and beady stuff wrapped around his wrists and neck. I had thought he was oddly dressed for someone seemingly interested in traditional theater. Daw Nge told me his name was Kaung Myat Aung but she called him Kaung Kaung.

Another boy about his same age, in his late teens, dressed as a monkey but without a mask, came after him, and opened a flat costume box. The punkish-looking boy took off his shirt, and the monkey began to help him dress in ogre's clothing: green shirt, green half-trousers with wide legs, and curvy, glittery green panels that covered his shoulders and wrists, with longer ones hanging from his shoulders. A scarf was tied around his waist and folded and tucked so that it flared to the sides. In front of two pairs of female eyes he changed without us having a glimpse of things females should not see. Actually, Daw Nge was not looking at him but I was, for I have an ogre puppet and wanted to see if the costume I had made for it was accurate.

After the boy was dressed, he took an ogre head from the table with both hands and reverently kissed it on the cheeks.

I was staring in astonishment at this when he slipped it on his head and oh my God—it was a terrifying moment to be sitting barely a foot away from a fully dressed ogre. I froze, my heart chilled to the core, and, with what little sense I had left, I managed to stop myself from shrieking the place down. I came out of my paralysis and could breathe once more only when he knelt down to adjust his cloth shoes, green and glittery with sequins.

Onstage for the first act, the boys became a monkey prancing merrily in a forest glade and an ogre checking his domain, who each came upon the other's footprints. As Kaung stalked and peered around with slow, menacing moves of his head, his fingers would clench into a fist, wrist turned downward, and then suddenly open with fingers gracefully arched, essential and beautiful parts of ogre choreography.

After he had made several turns around the stage to thunderous rolls of ogre music, he came face-to-face with the monkey. The monkey played the fool as they fought, but Good, of course, must triumph over Evil and the dance ended with the monkey winning the battle. What righteous lying crap, I muttered under my breath ... how can a monkey defeat an ogre? Besides, in reality, good has not triumphed over evil for, like what, ten thousand years?

While ogre and monkey chased and fought each other, Datha Giri, the ogre king, was getting dressed in "our" room. Powdering his face, he had no mirror so he used the mirror-covered blade of his sword. His costume was the same as Kaung's but he was well built and much taller which made him more imposing, especially when he put on his mask, after kissing it, of course. The high spike of his headdress made him look huge and evilly powerful, but luckily the earlier sight of ogre Kaung had immunized me against near-death terror.

After it was established that monkeys are Good and ogres Evil, the play officially began with a scene of an ogress praying to a hermit for sons and being told that her eldest would have ten heads (which would be one hard birth) and that one of her two other sons would be a good guy.

Another ogress took the stage, a good one called a Nat Belu or "celestial ogress," played by Thwe. She was trying hard to meditate but was interrupted again and again by Datha Giri hitting on her. He danced with extreme grace as he kept coming up to her and declaring his love, making gestures all the while to indicate what a lovely curvy body she had, which I daresay she found rather annoying. Finally in frustration she burned herself alive after cursing that she might in the next life be the death of him; it sounded like a universal curse uttered by many females, ogress or otherwise.

Then she was conceived in, and reborn from, a fang of Datha Giri, and no way in hell do I understand how. That's a problem for obstetricians to address. Because his court astrologers had predicted that the newborn baby would cause his death, Datha Giri placed her in an iron trunk which was buried in a paddy field. The king of Meikhtila held his annual plowing ceremony in that very same field and hit the trunk with his golden plow. When a baby girl was found inside, the childless king adopted her and named her Sita, with whom Datha Giri was to fall in love all over again, not realizing she was one born from his own tooth, a sort of orthodontic incest, one might say.

There was a deer's dance, and it was lovely to see Bambi dressed in gold and white as it capered, pranced, looked around nervously, and stepped daintily in a field of invisible, long stalks of grass that you knew was there solely by the way it walked. Then it scampered away from the hunter and finally, with a somersault, it disappeared into the bushes.

These and other scenes lasted almost the whole night, and there were no chairs backstage. When I sat on the floor my legs got numb; when I curled up to doze I missed scenes; when I was on my feet talking to the cast or taking photos, my legs ached so much they were just two pillars of throbbing pain that supported my weight.

By then Daw Nge was dressed; she took her ogress mask and kissed it on both cheeks before placing it over her head. The eye holes were rather small; how could anyone wearing this go out onstage, dance around, and not fall off the edge?

Her daughter was back and from their conversation I learned that Daw Nge had not been feeling well: she had asthma, and her daughter might have to sing her songs for her from behind the scenes. Her daughter scolded her gently for still wanting to perform in spite of her bad health, and Daw Nge smiled at her nattering. I could see that this tiny woman was not one to be swayed from something she wanted to do. A large number of females in my own circle of relatives are rather like that, looking as fragile as jasmine buds but made of stone.

On stage, the young princes Rama and Lekhana were placed under the care of the Bodaw, who would teach them the eighteen classical manly arts. The three of them, with two Po Thudaw, or servants of the monastery, were on their way through the woods, tree trunks and bushes on thin painted cloth that swayed gently in the draft that came up between the floorboards.

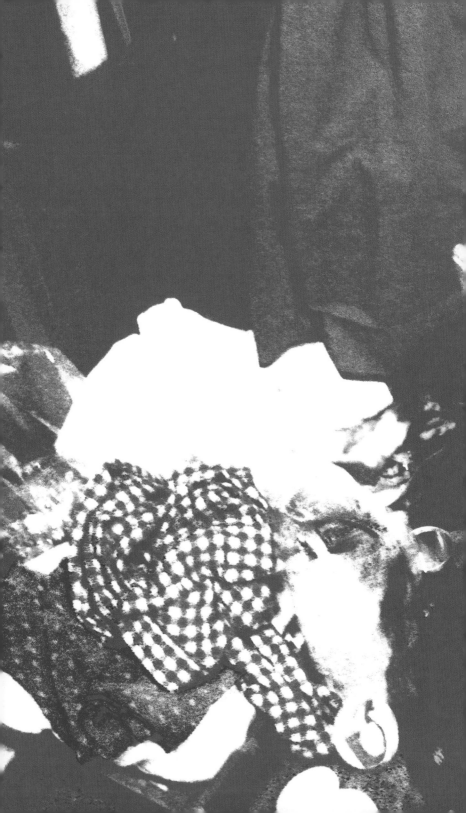

Daw Nge danced out onstage as the ogress Tataka, who was childless and wanted to adopt the princes. She rushed in to abduct them, but they managed to escape. As they rested, the Bodaw went off to meditate and told the Po Thudaw to take care of the boys. Tataka tracked them down and became aggressive in her pursuit whereupon, egged on by the Po Thudaw, young Rama shot and killed her.

During her death scene Daw Nge had to sing, but as she had been dancing all over the stage she was tired, and her voice faltered. Immediately her daughter took up the hand mike from backstage and continued the song in a very sweet voice *and* she could sing. Later when I complimented her, she told me yes, she could sing, but does not want to. Someone with a good voice who can sing, and does not want to? I was so jealous and annoyed with her waste of talent that I gave her the evil eye.

I knew what was coming in the night's finale, as I watched the adults who would play Rama and Lekhana make the final adjustments to their costumes. The young princes waded into the lake for a swim, and through the magical powers of the water they emerged as fully grown men.

To see the green and gold gods rising slowly and majestically out of the "lake" was showstopping. They helped each other descend from the bank of the lake, and marveled at how they were both transformed. I too, caught up in the magic of a shimmering golden god rising from the lake, marveled at Lekhana's beauty and stood rooted to my spot, completely enchanted. Probably my mouth was hanging open.

The scene ended with the grown-up princes and the Bodaw embracing each other tenderly. As the orchestra played the music of the show's end, I said goodbye to Daw Nge and told her I would see her tomorrow night. Oh no, she said, she had no scenes tomorrow and would rest at home.

In that case, I told her, I'm going home. I'd made friends with, and interviewed, most of the cast and those who were once members of the cast and those who hoped to be cast members in the future. I could not face being backstage another night without getting cozy with my newfound friend, this lovely ogress.

So I wished her well and before I left, I took Gambi's mask and gently kissed both cheeks.

CHAPTER FIFTEEN

Sardines on Board

I tumbled out of a trishaw, tottered up two flights of the inn's narrow, steep stairs, and toppled into bed before daybreak. I woke up an hour or so later, ate a snack without opening my eyes, and went back to sleep until almost noon. Then I washed up a bit, dragged a comb through my hair, and went downstairs to ask the hotel proprietor to please get me a cabin for the evening boat to Yangon.

At first I had thought I could travel home on the open deck but I had not brought any blankets, just a plastic sheet to lie on. The weather had been blazing hot and humid for days, but on the day that I decided to go home it suddenly became the coldest in the whole month of November. A stiff icy breeze cut across the river like a swirling razor of a kung fu hero, making its snaky way through my window. It got really chilly; I put on two extra blouses, topped them with my sweater, and decided to get a cabin, if I could.

By then, the manager was very respectful and helpful, having heard that this lone woman, with scandalous short hair and red lipstick, had really gone to see the Ramayana and came back at dawn actually from the Ramayana theater and had not been playing fast and loose someplace else.

When I asked him to get me a ticket for a cabin on the boat, the manager could not help himself. By car, he knew, it would take only four hours to get to the Dallah Jetty, and there a ferry ride across the river to Yangon's Strand Hotel would take five minutes. That same journey by boat from Pyapon would take me around eight hours, He had to ask softly and politely, his body bent almost double over his desk, "Elder Sister, why are you not going back by car?"

I told him I needed to check out the boat ride.

He promptly sent a boy off to buy a cabin ticket. It would be black market of course, since it was late in the day, so I handed the boy five thousand kyat.

"Tell the man at the ticket office that I sent you, it's for a very important guest from my inn," the manager called loudly after the boy. "Tell him to give my guest a clean room."

The boat was bright with fresh paint so I was not too worried about its cleanliness. After all, I thought, look where I was sleeping right now.

I could sense questions rattling around in the manager's head and he plucked at a polite one, asking with great deference if I was a teacher. I said no, smiled brightly at him without another word, went back to my room, and slept like a dead woman.

I was up by mid-afternoon, raging with thirst and hunger, and hastily took a cold shower to refresh myself. I went to the same restaurant as the day before where a row of shining steel pots waited on the counter, out of which I chose tender pork stew and some vegetables.

I was hungry and the food was good, and I made a contented hum as I ate. Either it pleased the girls that I enjoyed their food, or else they thought I was mad to hum while eating and were treating me gently, for when I told them to pack rice with fried prawns for my dinner, they gave me a large portion and added some fried roselle as a gift.

When I got back to the hotel, the manager told me that a cabin belonging to the butler had been booked for me at the cost of five thousand kyat, and that the boy from his hotel would escort me on board that evening. Apparently, since there were not enough cabins to go around, the crew often gave up their quarters to make some money. Good for them, I thought, in this time of high inflation; they were not stealing anything after all, but instead spent uncomfortable nights sleeping in the engine room.

At dusk I said goodbye to the manager and walked to the boat. I had naively thought that since going by car took a much shorter time, there would be plenty of room on board. I should have remembered that the boat was a triple-decker, and that they have this size because they need it.

The vessel was packed; people seemed to be sitting or lying in every available space—in the corridors, on deck, around the stairs, on the stairs, close to the railings, next to the loo. I had never seen a boat this crowded; it felt as if I'd stepped into a can of sardines.

I learned later that the ticket for sitting or sleeping on the deck was around five hundred kyat, and by car it would have cost about fifteen hundred. But it was not only the poor who were taking the river ride—I heard a snatch of conversation from the harried crew that about thirty doctors back from working in the

delta had taken over the salon under the bridge and that all the cabins were full of families, with at least five or six people in each. I saw that the wooden platforms for monks that were built about a foot off the deck were already occupied.

After finding the butler, I discovered that there had been a mix-up; his cabin had already been sold the day before. Okay, on the deck I was to be, but where? The boat by now looked like a white and blue overstuffed sardine can and probably the only space left was under the very boots of the captain in the wheelhouse. But I was lucky. The butler, apologizing profusely and looking very embarrassed, told me to wait while he tried to find another place. In ten minutes he was back, carrying a thick wool blanket and a pillow, both new-looking.

He took up my backpack with one hand and asked me to follow, walking toward the stern. He went around the back and entered a rather dingy room with two doors, one at either end, and two small windows. There was a broken TV high up against one wall and a battered sign hanging from the ceiling saying "Karaoke Lounge: one song 100 kyat, three for 200 kyat."

I was delighted that the TV was broken and even if it were not, I could not imagine that a karaoke session would work here. The room was already full of people, most lying down and already wrapped in cotton blankets like corpses. I saw no space for me, but my erstwhile host was keener of eye. He removed a few old plastic buckets and a dirty mop leaning against a wall next to a girl who was arranging her stuff around her, and there was my berth.

It was eighteen inches wide, I could see for sure, when I suddenly noticed a space marked in white paint on the wall where my head would be. The length was about four and a half feet, ending where it touched the side of a very narrow space: a path between the two tight rows of humanity lined up on either side of the room.

I am barely five feet two inches tall but if I stretched out, my feet would be scandalously entangled with the man's on the other side. I would have to sleep curled up like a fetus. Sighing in frustration, I silently took the blanket and pillow from my guide. I shook out the plastic sheet from my bag, placed the pillow against the wall, and folding the blanket so that it would be a soft, small mattress, laid it down where my back would be. With body heat steaming out from over thirty people packed into this room I thought I would not be chilly. My backpack I placed at the foot of my berth to make sure I would not be playing footsie in my sleep with strange men. I needn't have worried about that. Just before the boat departed, more people were lying, toe to head, along the path.

With a wall and a window on my right (Hallelooojah!), I made friends with the sardine on my left, young Zin Mar. She sold fruit in Pyapon and took a trip every three or four days to Yangon to stock up at the big wholesale fruit market. Her face looked a bit sulky, but only because of her full, beautiful lips (imagine Angelina Jolie's, only neater) and severe eyebrows. Her eyes were almond shaped, ringed with long lashes. Her face was thin so her cheekbones stood out; she had a very delicate and lovely bone structure. Her face looked as if it had been fashioned by an extremely patient sculptor.

I could see the same sort of face in her that you see in all those aloof international big-bucks-earning models looking down their noses from the catwalk, but her life was nothing like that. Since she was twelve, after she left school in the seventh grade, she had been a fruit seller. First she worked with her older cousin but four years later, she went solo. Now she was nineteen and earned enough to feed her parents.

"We're lucky here, Aunty," she said to me. Her smile was pretty but not on the scale of the knock-'em-dead one I'd seen on Gambi. "All the glass in the windows of the saloon is broken so in this weather it's going to be icy in there. On deck, too, it's going to be freezing ... some friends on the market wanted to save a bit so they're on deck. We'll meet up when we dock. We'll go home the same day that we get there, take the evening boat."

I thought of downtown Yangon with the posh shops and malls and wondered if she ever wanted to go there, but I realized before I asked that the one place any Buddhist would want to see in Yangon—even a young woman—is the Shwedagon Pagoda.

"While you're in Yangon, do you go to the pagoda?" I asked her.

"Oh, Aunty, I hardly have the time. We have to rush straight to the market, because the first load of fruit comes in by six in the morning. Then we just go back to the docks because we have to keep an eye on the fruit baskets or someone might grab an apple or two.

I can't afford that. But when someone among us offers to look after our stuff, then we get a chance for a quick prayer at the Shwedagon. It's not often, but I try to get there on my birthday."

Once they docked in Pyapon she let everyone else leave the boat so that she could get a porter and keep an eye on him when they disembarked.

"If there are crowds pushing to get off, I'd lose track of him, and sometimes they just leave the basket and try to look for other loads to carry. By the time I get to my things or when they come back for payment, a few pieces of fruit might be missing."

By then we had been on the water for a couple of hours, and I had dinner while Zin Mar ate sweet pancakes with tea from a plastic bottle she had brought along. She refused my offer to share my rice, saying she'd eaten at home. I hoped it was true.

I told her I had been at the Ramayana last night and she said she had gone there last year to sell fruit at the night bazaar, but not this year. When I observed that the night bazaar was so crowded I could hardly move through it, she laughed out loud.

"Oh Aunty, you should see Independence Day. It's so crowded you're sort of carried along, tightly squeezed between bodies. I always lose my slippers; but sometimes I'd go back to the place where I'd noticed them dropping off and if I look around, sometimes I get them back. The sides of the streets are just lined with slippers!"

I was amazed. In Yangon there were celebrations on that day of January 4 and every neighborhood observed it with footraces, games, football matches, and other events. That was about all, as far as I'd noticed. What went on in Pyapon, and who came?

"Villagers from all around come and they stay the night," Zin Mar explained. "They rent a large boat and the whole village arrives in the morning, or families come in their small boats. The riverside is jammed with boats. They do some shopping, there are special shops from the government with stuff from factories; they sell pots and pans or soap or cotton longyi or biscuits or orange squash or medicine. Then we always have a baby show, and the fattest babies get prizes! There's a vegetable show and people enter their biggest eggplants or gourds, or those growing in strange shapes. We like that part; my friends and I head there first."

"That's it for the whole day?" I asked.

"Well, there are Ferris wheels and merry-go-rounds, and so many things to eat. In the evening there's a Zat Pwe theater and everyone watches all night and goes home early the next morning. It's such fun!"

She laughed again, perhaps seeing it all in her mind. She sounded utterly happy.

I am constantly amazed at the simple wants and contentment of rural people. I have heard almost the same thing from up-country villagers, but here, just hours away from the biggest city in the country, a pretty girl could still be delighted with vegetables twisted into odd shapes.

Just then the boat tooted and slowed, and we docked at Kyait Lat. There was a crowd of about a hundred people waiting to board, with our poor boat already stuffed to capacity. Zin Mar went off to see her friends and I curled up for a snooze.

Suddenly I heard shouts, rolled over, and got up on my feet, clutching at my longyi to make sure it was not left behind on my "bed." I peered out of the window and saw some baskets of flowers floating by very quickly in the fast current, speeding past so fast that in seconds they were out of sight. Some men jumped in and they too disappeared after the baskets. I felt alarmed and miserable; they'd surely drown for a few baskets of flowers they had no hope of catching. The current was just too fast. I lay back, trying not to think of these men, their bodies washed out to sea, their wives and children ...

Some men outside our karaoke room were talking about a

small boat carrying flowers that our boat had rammed.

I did not feel like getting up from my fetal position for the entire hour that we were in Kyait Lat. I got up only when we left, as Zin Mar came back. She said she'd been up to the prow to see what had happened.

No, it wasn't another boat we sank, it was a pile of flower baskets placed too near the rail that had toppled over when new passengers surged on board. I asked about the men in the river, but she assured me that hereabouts people are constantly dipping into fast-flowing waters like this—yes, even at night, if they have to go after an escaping boat or something.

"Don't worry, Aunty," she said, shaking her head with a smile, "most of us grow up like fish."

"Aha!" I replied, finally having the heart to joke. "So you're a mermaid, eh? Knew it."

I awoke when it was still dark to go to the loo, a necessity that I dreaded since it was a very, very crowded ship; would the toilets be clean? Glory be, they were. As I walked there and back, I had to step carefully around sleeping bodies on the open deck, wrapped against the cold in blankets or sometimes only their longyi.

I turned a corner toward our cabin, gasped in awe, and nearly stepped on someone's head. There was the Shwedagon Pagoda a long way off, lit up with lights, a shimmering mountain of gold. I was surrounded by a velvety, dark blue, but faint outline that let me know we must be in the Twanté Canal. I had seen the Shwedagon from this point in daylight and had thought how majestic it looked looming over the Yangon skyline, but now, in the dark and shining like a beacon, it was magnificent.

I gazed and gazed until the cold drove me inside. Zin Mar was asleep, her hands over her belly, and I noticed that her hands were lovely too. Her fingers were smoothly tapered and long, and I wished silently that one day she might have rubies and diamonds on them instead of the thin gold band she was wearing.

By the first light of dawn we were approaching Yangon. I chatted with Zin Mar for the last time, happy to have met her, both of us knowing our paths would probably not cross again. I got my stuff ready and stepped outside.

And I saw a pink Yangon.

The water, the high-rises, the docks, the ships, the sampans, the sky, everything was a dusky pink and I fell in love all over again with my city.

CHAPTER SIXTEEN

My Pretty Pathein Girl

To go from Yangon to the sea, for the final run of my river ride, I could easily drive to a town on the river and then hire a sampan to take me out to sea, only a thirty-minute excursion. Or I could go to the jetty opposite the Strand Hotel, pay a boatman to row me out to sea, and that would be the end of my journey. Both of these possibilities seemed unworthy of the Ayeyarwaddy.

There is one place I had never been to, the southwestern tip of the country that looks out toward the Indian Ocean. Called Cape Nagris by the British, we know it as Mawtin Zun, zun meaning spur. Not surprisingly, there is nothing much there but a pagoda at the very tip of the spur, standing isolated and abandoned most of the year and coming alive with its festival in February. I was determined to see this pagoda, and from the beach look south to the Indian Ocean, vast and uninterrupted by land until Antarctica, or southeast toward Australia where a few school friends now live, or southwest toward India, Africa, and South America, places I long to see.

After my decision to go to Mawtin Zun, the first thing I packed was the compass I had found some time ago in the Yangon street stall. I wanted to be damn sure I would be facing in the direction of Peru while yearning for its parrots and orchids, and not looking toward Australia and its kangaroos.

By mid-January I began to plan the Mawtin Zun trip, with the help of Ma Hlaing who had gone there the year before. Special triple-decker boats for the festival would leave beginning on the twenty-third of February, the first day of the celebration. My departure was on the twenty-fifth and I was all packed and ready a week before that date. I only needed to get my ticket, which Ma Hlaing's husband Kyaw would procure for me.

Both he and Ma Hlaing were worried that I insisted on going alone; they wanted to send someone, a girl from their furniture shop perhaps, to look after me. They wanted to pack enough food so that I would not have to eat at the food stall on board. They were determined to get me a cabin so that I would not have to sleep on deck. Their tender hearts could not stand for anybody they knew—not only me—to be in discomfort.

But worse was to come.

A week before my departure they saw in a weekly paper that someone from the meteorology department had said a cyclone with speeds of over one hundred miles per hour might hit us again around the end of February. They were frantic with worry when they told me the news.

All that night I thought of the horror of Cyclone Nargis when it had struck the previous May. Was I going to meet a watery end? Drowned dead and washed out to sea and perhaps back to shore? Good God, would my body be starkers when it was recovered? Should I make sure that I had on new and durable underwear at all times? Should I even risk this journey? But, I argued internally, the festival would last only fifteen days, and storms might hit in other years as well, at any time. I could not make up my mind whether to go or not.

I have often thought about how terrifying it must have been for those who died in the tidal wave during Nargis, and now I thought of myself facing the same fate. I'd done what I wanted practically my whole life and would hate to live to a tottering, helpless, ripe old age, so I wasn't really afraid to die. After all, a lot of friends, lovers, and family, many of whom truly, deeply loved me, had Gone Beyond and they might be there to welcome me. If so, I could not be happier. But if I died away from Yangon, it might cause problems for my living friends, who would be unable to get into my flat and wouldn't even be sure I was really dead.

I drove the next morning to Ma Hlaing's place, where I read every word of the article. It gave a list of rivers in the delta where boats should moor during a storm, which had freaked her out. However, the good news was that they were talking about a particular type of storm which they said usually only hits the far north. I was headed south, so at once I decided I would go.

First I had to promise Ma Hlaing that at any sight of a grey cloud I would not step on board any boats or go wandering around the delta, but would come straight home.

Four days later, Ma Hlaing called me early in the morning. Apparently another news source checked with the meteorological department and was told this was all a misunderstanding—the storm was expected in May, not in February.

Great relief was felt all around, especially by friends whom I'd promised to haunt after I died—not out of malice but with a purely scientific intent to let them know what lies beyond, although many of them seemed somewhat uninterested in the answer. Probably it would not have worked, for I'd had a similar pact with my uncle U Win Maung, who had done research on reincarnation and who passed away in 1990. Either he lost all memory of his promise or he could not get in touch with me since I was in prison at the time for political reasons. Maybe the high black walls of Insein Prison were guarded by malevolent beings that prevented him from reaching me.

Now that the misunderstanding was cleared up, I began to pack comfort food—packets of instant lemon tea and bags of potato chips. Ma Hlaing insisted on providing food for my meals since the boat would leave at 3 p.m. and would not arrive until the following afternoon, a journey of over twenty-four hours. She and Kyaw would fetch me at 2 p.m. and see me safely on board. They had booked one whole cabin for me instead of only one berth, for they knew I liked to be on my own.

I was all dressed and ready to go by noon. They arrived promptly at two. Their car was loaded with stuff for me: bottled water, oranges, cookies, and boxes that contained rice, steamed vegetables, fried creamed corn, fried roselle leaves, roast chicken and ... oh yum ... grilled pork ribs. That very night in my cabin I would be enjoying ribs with lemon tea, I vowed silently.

"I hope the food lasts until you get to the festival," Ma Hlaing commented, knowing me well. "I hope I packed enough."

I assured her it was enough to feed all the passengers. She reminded me not to eat clams or oysters because in this heat they might not be fresh and could make me sick. I kept silent; no way was I going to promise not to eat oysters.

They saw me to my cabin and Ma Hlaing handed me a lime.

"This was blessed by our monk especially for you," she said. "Keep it in your bag at all times; it will protect you from harm."

"*What* harm?" I wailed. "I'll be *fine*, it's a *pagoda* festival, don't *worry*, and I promise to come straight *home*."

Then, remembering that my lemon tea was not as tart as I liked, I asked, "Can I use this in my tea?"

"Yes, of course," said Kyaw and "*No, you can't!*" said Ma Hlaing, simultaneously.

Kyaw immediately shut his lips, throwing his wife an adoring, apologetic glance.

"Wouldn't it be better if it were actually in *me* and not in my bag?" I argued, but when I saw her giving me her look, I meekly said I would bring back the whole undamaged lime to show her.

As they left, Ma Hlaing kept turning around to look back at me with some anxiety.

"Be good and phone me as soon as you get there," she said.

I called after her that I would behave myself.

My cabin was small but clean, with two berths against the inner wall and a table between them that held a fan. Soon after I was settled in, the other passengers arrived but it seemed the upper-class cabins were none too full.

"Not to worry," said a cabin boy when I commented on this, "we'll be making a few stops and getting more passengers on the way."

In the next cabin was a married couple. The husband, who looked about sixty, was slim, tall, and spry. I could not guess the age of the wife, whose name I later learned was Myaing, "Forest." She was somewhat plump (oh well, fat), but graceful and light on her feet, with daintily small wrists and ankles. Her complexion was a perfect gold-brown. Being overweight had made her face full, as were her lips which were a soft pink color. I could not see her eyes behind her large round sunglasses. She wore a dusky pink blouse-and-pants outfit, and the color made her skin glow. I was surprised at how good she looked, even with the immensity of her size.

For some months I had noticed that my school chums who put on weight actually managed to look really attractive, with elegant clothes and accessories, careful makeup, and tasteful colors. Those who kept very slim also looked nice but only from a distance; their faces were often ravaged with deep lines. My neighbor on the boat was undeniably huge but she looked wonderful and much younger than her years. I thought she was in her thirties, but she said her children were already grown and married.

I felt pleased with this: I now had proof that even if women got overly fat in their mature years, they could still look great. I felt that if men of our age have eyes only for young, slim bodies with spectacular boobs, let them: we could feel good about ourselves without needing confirmation from men of any age. (But if these men who looked at younger women happened to be our husbands, bash 'em one, I say.)

On my other side was a young family; the father hardly seemed out of his teens. Walking the deck in front of our cabins, he would jiggle and toss his six-month-old baby girl, and I was terrified that he would jiggle her too enthusiastically and drop her overboard.

At exactly three o'clock we were off to a '60s song of "My Pretty Pathein Girl," since the biggest town nearest Mawtin Zun is Pathein or Bassein. The singer, Tin Oo Lay, was a young teen at the time, and he sang in his sweet treble about an older Pathein girl who was almost like his elder sister. It was a favorite song of the delta. Ma Hlaing had warned me that I would hear it many times on my trip and so I kept count—fourteen renditions. When we slowed down to dock at each stop, the song would blare out, either sung or played on a synthesizer or issuing from a traditional orchestra of drums, oboe, and gongs.

The music lent a festive air to the boat and so did plastic bags: our boat was decorated with pale blue, pink, and yellow bags cut into strips and hung along the edge of the decks. On the open top deck the crew had left the bags uncut so that they filled out and

looked like lines of pastel balloons. They swooshed and swished in the breeze, sounding like bamboo leaves in a storm.

We passed little villages or isolated huts built right on the river, a private bamboo "jetty" jutting out into the water. Naked children playing in the water or up in trees or leaning out of windows watched us pass and waved energetically. As we went down the Twanté Canal, I saw the same white-plastic roofed huts I had seen on my way to Pyay.

At Twanté I saw an imposing, three-storied brick house with tall Greek pillars and blue-glassed windows standing between wooden shacks with tin roofs, right on the river. Away from the center of town

there were hulks of damaged ships dragged up to shore for possible repairs; some did not look as if they would ever be seaworthy again. But then, Myanmar's mechanics are great with keeping things going ... some of our buses are pre-World War II Chevrolets, with large holes in the dusty, grimy wooden flooring, their gear sticks long replaced with wooden two-by-fours.

By evening of the first day we reached Maubin. I had heard of the monstrous mosquitoes of that town so I kept my cabin door closed the whole time we were docked there. I could hear vendors from the jetty hawking rice and curry, grilled fish, sticky rice cakes, and other dishes. I had dinner from the boxes Ma Hlaing had given me, especially relishing the succulent chicken and fried creamed corn, soft and sweet.

When we cast off, I was ready for a bath of cool but brownish river water. Afterward it was a bit chilly on deck as Myaing and I leaned on the railings for a chat. She and her husband, with their children all grown and settled, were able to travel and this they had been doing for the past five years. They had gone several times over to all the famous pilgrimage sites of the country. This trip was their fourth time to Mawtin Zun.

"The first time we came," she said, "I fed the dragon and made a wish, and it came true! So since then we come every year."

Feeding a dragon? This was news to me. In our myths dragons, "naga," are water-dwelling serpents, with the power to change to any size or into human form. Their bodies are scaly and green and their crested heads are made of gold, as are their tails. Their fiery breath can burn you to a crisp.

Myaing said the food customarily offered to the dragon is milk and popped rice. To my mind this was rather bland fare for a fire-breathing serpent, but I supposed whole barbecued cows would be beyond the means of most pilgrims. I asked her where she managed to find milk.

"There are shops that sell ready-prepared bowls of milk and

popped rice," she said, "small plastic bowls that you float off from the spur leading out to sea."

The second time she came here, she confided, she had been so eager to offer the dragon the very best of fare that she had brought a can of evaporated milk and popped corn with her from Yangon. I could understand this: popped rice tastes like Styrofoam.

"I filled the bowl almost to the brim, and it sank," she ended sadly.

"You know, the dragon king lives under the sea so it probably landed at his feet," I said, and her face brightened.

"There are three walkways to the pagoda," she then told me. "One is on the southeast for the Weikza, the ascetics who live in the region or who fly in from other places on their pilgrimage rounds. Then, on the southwest, directly in line with a small pagoda and the spire where you float off the dragon king's food, is the walkway that the dragons use when they come to pray. And the last one on the south is where the wild elephants come."

Wild elephants? In this hilly region of empty scrubland and thick woods I could easily visualize roaming herds of wild elephants, since I knew that we have a lot of them in the delta and in the jungles along the western coastline. I remarked that it would be great to see dragons, Weikza, or at the very least wild elephants.

"Oh no," Myaing said. "They never come during festival time, not even the elephants. The day after the festival ends and everyone has gone, the tide rises right up to the foot of the hill and washes away all the garbage and dirt. Only then do they come to pray."

So, anyone who stayed behind to check them out would be washed away as well—so much for research.

It was getting cold so we parted, I to nibble grilled ribs for my supper while sipping lemon tea and rereading Anthony Bourdain's *A Cook's Tour,* which I had brought with me. I fell into a deep sleep, satiated with ribs and—more vicariously—with Bourdain's fantastic meals.

The half-disc sun rose out of dusky mauve-grey clouds when we docked at Maubin the next morning. It was so foggy that we had to wait some time to be on our way, but soon the mist was driven away by the cold, early-morning light that shone on the water, turning it into patches of beaten silver.

By early afternoon we were in Pathein. It was hideously hot, for my cabin was on the west side, but it would have been worse on shore under the blazing sun. We stopped for over an hour there, and Myaing and her husband hopped off to eat lunch.

"The prawn curries here are the best," they said.

I lay gasping for air in my cabin. With the engines off I could not turn on my fan.

From Pathein it was down south along the wide and straight Pathein River. In ancient times the Pathein River was one of the two entry routes for seafaring ships coming to the old Pyu city of Srikhetera, to Bagan, or to Bago, once the great royal capital of King Bayint Naung, founder of the Third Myanmar Empire. The other route was up the Yangon River, which lies further east and is now the main port for international ships to dock.

I wondered if instead of Yangon, Pathein could become the main port of Myanmar again; that would clear up the ugly warehouses along Yangon's Strand Road, and would allow them to be replaced with a long stretch of riverfront. There could be parks, meditation gardens, outdoor art galleries, open-air cafés, craft shops, space for free puppet shows, all surrounded by rows of stalls

cooking traditional snacks like pancakes. Every day would be a street fair. I dream, oh how I dream ...

By 4 p.m. we were passing Haing Gyi Kyun, a large island taken over by the navy, with a hill rising out of the otherwise flat land in the shape of a bull elephant's back ... bull elephants are called "haing." We took a shortcut through a channel between this island and the mainland and turned westward to make a final stop at Kha Maut Maw, a fishing village.

Along the route were acres of dhani, or nipa, palms reaching the horizon. Their frondlike leaves, rising straight out of the roots, are used to make roofs that last at least three years. Just after the storm, when new huts needed to be built and roofed, there was no dhani to be had but now the ones I saw would be ready for harvest in a couple of weeks. This was fortunate, because plastic sheets might be useful for roofs but make the interior of the houses extremely hot.

As the sun was beginning to set we arrived at Kha Maut Maw. It was a mad scramble to get a taxi—small motorcycles which take passengers on the backseat and their luggage between the knees of the driver. Myaing hastily told me exactly where we would meet; we were going to stay at a guesthouse with small bamboo rooms, smack in the middle of the festival shops.

Within minutes we were away, riding along the beach toward a spectacular sunset, a wide swath of crimson running across the sky under and around a mass of steely grey clouds.

CHAPTER SEVENTEEN
Feeding the Dragon

On our way to our guesthouse, we passed through Kan Chaing, a very clean and neat "long" village: one in which all the houses are set up along the main road, with none placed behind them. We were going slowly, as Myaing before leaving had called to my driver to be careful of her "elder sister."

The driver told me he was from this village when I commented on its cleanliness. I hesitated, then asked him how he had fared during Cyclone Nargis.

"We lost everything, Aunty," he said. "Only this bike was left." Those living near the sea had been washed away, he told me, whole houses with whole families.

I asked him if he had known the storm was coming and he said yes, they were warned the day before. I wanted to know if they heard the warning on the radio or on TV, but he said they didn't have TV and few of them listened to the radio. However, the navy boats sent from Haing Gyi Kyun warned them from loudspeakers, telling the villagers to leave everything and go up to higher ground.

"But we had never had any storm like this before and could not believe it would be really dangerous. Besides, people did not want to leave their houses or things ..."

Although Myaing had told my motorcycle man to take me to the bamboo guesthouse, he took me to the one with wooden huts, obviously considering it a better choice. It looked gloomy and rather dilapidated, without the gentle appearance of bamboo mats as walls, which I prefer. So I insisted that he take me to the right place and we stalked off, this time on foot, my driver carrying my bags. The manager of these wooden horrors, from the same family that owned the bamboo huts, was left muttering to himself that he had never heard of anyone favoring bamboo over wood—liar.

We soon arrived at the bamboo guesthouse where Myaing and her husband were sitting in easy chairs near the front desk, which was a small table on the bare ground. Behind them I could see a large bamboo hall separated into rooms by bamboo mats. They were delighted to see me and introduced me to the manager, Ko Cho Aye or "Sweetly Cool." Since this is a name more appropriate for a cute girl, he looked embarrassed, but what gave me a shock was that he looked exactly like the manager of the other place I had left minutes ago. For the first few seconds I had thought the other chap had somehow taken a shortcut to arrive here before me. That was Sweetly Cool's younger brother, I discovered later, but not his twin.

I was shown to my room, which was usually six thousand kyat a night, but as I was Myaing's friend, I was given it for five thousand. It had a dirt floor with a large bamboo platform as a bed for however many guests wanted to fit in the room. The platform was so big that it was a struggle for me to get in and close the door.

I dumped my bags and galloped back out, running past Myaing and her husband as I called to them that I must go to the pagoda.

It was hard going, walking across pits of sand, but I managed to reach the pagoda without too much exertion. I went puffing and huffing up the Elephants' Walk, which had very wide steps built presumably for feet bigger than those of humans.

Suddenly, as soon as I stepped on the pagoda platform, my exhaustion ceased as if by magic. I found myself breathing naturally, my heart beating at its normal unnoticeable pace. Could it be the power of the dragon?

The pagoda was well kept with marble tiles on the floor and fresh gold on the spire, which was almost the same design as that of the Shwedagon. The flower sellers told me it was not unduly damaged

in the storm, that it possesses too much glory for any storm to come near it.

I walked around the narrow platform, thinking how marvelous it would be if I could see the elephants, the Weikza, and the dragons jostling for elbow room to sit and pray, once we human intruders left their place. Surely the dragons would change into human form, or else their slithering bodies might be trampled by the elephants. The Weikza, with their ability to fly, would hover above them all, praying aloft in privacy.

The next morning I was up early and feeling groggy. The previous night I was fast asleep and snoring happily by 8 p.m. However, from eleven onward, two all-night video halls, one on each side of the guesthouse, had played one unbelievably bad movie after the other. The stupid jokes and the raucous forced laughter of the actors had me writhing in bed and grinding my teeth in fury until dawn.

After reviving over breakfast, I decided to explore. Ma Hlaing had told me about a good beach about seven miles away by motorbike taxi, called Ngwe Taung or "Silver Hill," originally Mwe Taung or "Snake Hill." (Dragons and snakes seemed to have had some importance in the old days.) I hailed a bike and off we went.

It was a pleasant ride, and the Ngwe Taung beach was nice enough, with of course a small pagoda on another rocky spur. A row of shops sat silent and completely without customers; they had an air of barely stifled impatience. I walked up to one to buy a bottle of water and asked the lady there if the pagoda here had any connections to magical dragons. She said no, so I decided not to go see it. In a few days this beach would be hopping, but very few pilgrims were there now, and most of them were like me, wanting to escape the crowds.

On our way back I saw two fishermen and a dog pulling in a very long net. Actually the men were pulling, with the dog giving them moral support, running from one to the other. We stopped and

I hopped off, running toward the man closest to me ... I was determined to get some lovely photos of pretty silvery fish.

The other man was a long distance away and the two walked slowly toward each other as they dragged the net ashore. The man near me was pulling really hard and I was sure they must have a heavy catch. They finally pulled up the whole net onto the sand and in it were five small fish, one dead.

A fish flopped onto the beach and the dog ate it. Feeling very sorry for the fishermen, I watched them roll up the net to try again some yards away.

I plopped down on the sand, thinking what a damn hard life it was to drag this net out to sea and drag it back again, just for five fish, one dead. As I sat there three young monks and a boy passed behind me on foot. I scrambled up and ran after them to donate four thousand kyat. "For the morning meal," I said, handing the cash to the boy with both hands.

Perhaps my donation was a reaction to the meager catch I had witnessed, but I couldn't offer money to the fishermen. It would have insulted them, although God knows they must have needed it desperately. I had no idea what to do.

The taxi rider must have guessed how I felt, for he told me that fishing was hit-or-miss and in another place a school of fish might just swim into the men's nets. To distract me he said that he had fought to be able to come to this festival, for he lives in Pathein and must, must, must come every year.

"Not to fool around, no, Aunty," he said, looking far too innocent. "I just want to pray and make some extra cash is all."

(Hmm, I thought, since festivals like this one are where young men come to meet pretty girls from other parts of the country.)

Last year he had to do some errands for his mum in other towns and had missed the whole show. A month ago, he told me, he had announced to his family that this year he was not going to do any

errands for anybody.

"Of course I didn't dare to address this to Mum directly," he said. "She'd have taken my head off."

I went back to the stalls near our guesthouse, looking for gifts for my friends. Wendy wanted fish paste, but I heard that this could be sandy if the sellers had dried the fish on the beach. After meandering indecisively from one end of the long rows to the other, I bought bags of dried shrimp instead.

Then I spotted a harness shop and remembered I had to buy some "jingle" harness bells, the spherical ones we call "chu."

I used to have a small cowbell with a distinct sound on my front door for times when there were power cuts and the electric bell didn't work, but then some sleazebag stole it. I replaced it with an ordinary bell, but my neighbors had the same kind so I never realized anyone was at my front door jangling away until they began to scream my name.

The chu makes a distinctive sound so I thought that if I had several, hung out of reach from outside but with a string to pull them, it might be easy for me to hear them ring. I bought six large ones, which are usually used to decorate bullocks' harnesses on special occasions. The young man selling it wanted to know exactly how I would use it, so I had to explain everything. I think he wanted a new sales pitch to use on other customers.

I went back to the guesthouse, unloaded my goods, and ate the final leftovers from Ma Hlaing's care parcel. Then I walked over to the small pagoda on the spur. If the dragon king observed Buddhist precepts, he would not eat after the noon hour. It was now just after eleven so I still had time to offer him food.

A long concrete walkway led over the jagged rocks, and at the other end near the pagoda steps were shops. I only saw flowers and small terra-cotta vases with colorful paper banners and umbrellas for sale, so I asked where I might buy milk for the dragon.

"Here. We have it," a younger woman inside the stall said and showed me a plastic bowl of milk and a bag of popped rice, which she opened and mixed into the milk. I asked how and where I should feed the dragon.

"Just go down to the end of the spur," she said, pointing out to sea, "and float it on the water."

I climbed up to the pagoda platform. From the side leading to the spur there were boulders stacked like steps. I was afraid that if I slipped on them I would be drenched with milk and, as I hesitated, a young photographer came up and took the bowl from my hands.

"I'll help you get there, Aunty," he said. He held my bowl with one hand and my elbow with the other while I made my shaky way over wet boulders right up to the very end of the spur. Other pilgrims had already made their wishes and were now on their way back so I was alone, for my young helper walked a few steps away to give me privacy.

There was a smooth place just big enough for me to kneel. I placed the bowl of milk and popped rice in front of me on a smaller rock and closed my eyes, but not so tightly that I wouldn't be able to spot a gold-crested creature should he arise from the sea.

So, there I was. What would I wish for? I wasn't sure I could make a string of wishes, so right now what was most urgently needed in my life? There was a publisher who had dragged his feet over three of my manuscripts for more than four years by now—should I ask the dragon to go see him, maybe breathe on him a little? But then, since I am very fond of his wife, I thought I should pray for something else.

Other than an unrealistic wish for a million dollars to start my own publishing house—might as well ask for the moon to fall on my lap—what did I really need?

Then I got it.

I shut my eyes tight, placed my clasped hands on my forehead, carefully chose the words I had to say, and then recited them very slowly and firmly:

"Please, King of the Dragons, with all your majestic powers, please protect our shores. Please never allow a storm like Nargis to destroy any part of our land ever again. Use your powers to grow to a gigantic size and let your body bar the winds. Blow your fiery breath into the cyclones and turn them away. Please, save us. Please."

I knelt in silence for a few seconds and bowed three times. I set the bowl gently on the soft waves and watched it float away. I felt ... not assured exactly, but hopeful. Very hopeful.

CHAPTER EIGHTEEN

End of My River

I was ready for a nap after my walk back from the spur; I could see my shadow wobbling all over the sand, looking drunk. I went into my room but it was too hot to stay there. All of the rooms were packed into a very large hall and although there was ample space between the top of the walls and the ceiling, there were no windows. The sun was directly overhead and long, thin rods of light fell through the holes in the bamboo matting of the roof, making my gloomy room look like a spectacular art installation. But I could not lie there basking in art while being roasted to a crisp. I felt desperate ... where was I to go?

Then I noticed that the corridors were good wind tunnels so I went out to sit in one of the easy chairs by the "front desk," moving it to be almost in the intersection of two corridors so I could get the breeze from both directions. However, if I had hoped to make up for the night before with some drowsy downtime, I was mistaken. A group of guests had arrived while I was away and some of them were in the lobby, sitting on easy chairs or mats. One or two taxi riders, friends of Sweetly Cool, were also hanging around since in the hot afternoon they had no passengers.

But their conversation was miles better than the inane scripts of the all-night movies. I pretended not to listen but soon gave up the farce because I couldn't keep a straight face. "Sweetly Cool" Ko Cho Aye did better than I, as he probably has sat at his desk for years listening to his countrymen in holiday mood, but his lips were twitching.

"If I should cry, my tears would be the size of pumpkins," whined one rider. Asked why, he said that morning he had lent his motorcycle to two boys, friends of his kid brother. They had taken it out on a spin and brought it back without its back license plate and missing a mudguard. They had no idea where these things had fallen off.

"Not only that," our chap moaned, "when they returned my bike they nearly ran into Daw Ma Gwe, you know that old lady who sells burn-tongue noodles?"

Indeed they all knew her, a fierce woman with a bad temper. Burn-tongue is a very apt name for the dish that she sold, which has two types of chili paste added to noodles that have already been cooked with enough chilies to tear out your throat and tongue.

"Nothing happened to her but she scolded me for half an hour; the kids just ran off when they saw her face."

He vowed to strangle his brother as soon as he got home. We laughed that in all this mess, everyone got punished but the two culprits.

The new guests had arrived by "speed boats," small, fast ferry boats plying between Pathein and Mawtin Zun, named—oh what else for God's sakes—Pathein Girl One through Four. These guests were going back the next day, for not many pilgrims spend more than two nights here, and they were booking their tickets with the company agent who makes personal calls to guesthouses.

"So we are going back on Pathein Girl Two, are we?" asked one man who looked as though he was in his late thirties. "Can't we go on Pathein Girl One? We came on that."

The agent replied that it was Pathein Girl Two's turn to make the trip tomorrow. Then the man asked if the girl staff of each Pathein Girl boat stayed put on their boats or moved around. The agent said that PG One girls stayed on PG One and PG Two girls stayed on PG Two. Always, he added firmly.

I was wondering why the PG One girls were special, until the passenger explained it to the whole audience at large, for by then everyone was listening intently. (We Myanmar people don't usually hide our interest in other people's business; we actually pay them a compliment by being interested, don't we?)

It seemed that on the way here he had made friends with the pretty staff of PG One, but it had taken him and his two friends over twenty thousand kyat worth of beer to get up the courage to ask their names.

"So we already know them," he moaned. "On the way back the new girls won't know us so it's going to cost us another twenty thousand."

Myaing and her husband turned up; they too had been feeding the dragon. They were leaving to catch a speedboat that would take them to Pathein before they returned home to Yangon. We said goodbye, and I thanked them for looking after me. As they left on the backs of motorbikes I thought of them in the coming years traveling from place to place, going over and over to famous pilgrimage sites, looking after each other gently and lovingly. When they came here next year, I hoped they would think of me.

The other guests got ready to go to the pagoda, feed the dragon, and shop-shop-shop. I was left with the two bike riders who were sleeping on easy chairs and Sweetly Cool who sat at his desk.

One rider woke up and told me about the time a long, thin snake had come to the pagoda during festival time. It lay on the ground by the side of the southwestern steps, its body straight, looking up at the pagoda.

"Its tail and head were lifted off the ground, just like the concrete model of the dragon on the stairs," he said. I had not noticed it but knew that was the one typical pose of painted or sculpted dragons.

Then Ko Cho Aye, a bit hesitantly and eyeing me shyly in case I started hooting with laughter, began a story that had happened several years before when a long smear of something that smelled fishy had been discovered on the pagoda platform one morning at dawn, days before the festival started, while he and others were still building their huts and shops.

"There was nothing on the steps of the dragon's walkway but from the top of it, and all around the spire, there was a greasy smear on the tiles. It looked as if a wide body had slithered around, with its smear stopping when it got back to the same steps again. We scraped off a bit and smelled it, and it smelled fishy, but our fishermen friends told us it was not exactly like the smell of a fish."

Everyone was convinced that a dragon—was it His Majesty?—had made a visit, climbing the steps in human form but preferring to pray in his natural state.

I was intrigued and not at all in the mood to laugh. I was writhing inside with envy that I had not been there and that no serpents came to pray this year, right now. Was it an emergency that caused the Dragon King not to wait for the festival to end? Or did he get his dates mixed up? That I could understand and sympathize with.

Dammit, I thought, I wish I could meet him in any form, serpent or human. I wondered what he would look like as a man. Very handsome, I bet, with sleek black hair combed back from his face. He would be graceful with a trim but muscled body, icy-cold black eyes, and well-shaped thin lips. Or was I thinking of Al Pacino in *Godfather I*?

"By the way, Aunty," Ko Cho Aye said to me, "you might be interested in the moving grass."

I pricked my ears; I had read somewhere a long time ago about a certain type of vine that grew on our western coastline and moved around as if it were a living creature. But grass? I could get no more information out of Ko Cho Aye other than that he had heard of an old man who sells it at the Well of Celestials, on the other side of a hill farther back from the beach. He did not know how the grass showed that it could move; he had only heard its name, myet shin.

He gave me explicit directions on how to get to the well, adding that people believe that its water is miraculous and bring empty bottles with them to fill and take home. I was only interested in the grass, however.

"It's still too hot, Aunty," he said. "You can go later. I'll send one of my boys with you."

I said I was used to tramping around all by myself, I'd be fine.

"Well, it's really isolated, there are only one or two families living around there. I'd much rather send someone with you."

We argued gently until I convinced him that I'd be fine on my own and headed off to check out the moving grass.

The hill in front of which the grass was supposed to be sold was rather a long way off, and I strode determinedly over sand which sucked in my feet and made it hard to walk. Ko Cho Aye stood on the beach looking after me, brow scrunched in anxiety.

Once I reached the hill I had to walk up a steep, winding lane, then up a flight of steps that were even steeper, over small pebbles in my bare feet since I was then near the spire of a pagoda, and then along a dirt lane … slippers on again … that wound between high bushes.

There I came upon a drying, but not entirely dry, mound of elephant poo. Trust me, I know cow dung and that was not it. Not much farther ahead I could see bushes by the side that were trampled and flattened as if something large had made its way through them to get to this lane.

I stood still, heart thumping like mad. I thought frantically about what I should do if I turned a corner and came face-to-face with a wild elephant, forgetting in my terror that the poo was not fresh. I knew that while walking in the woods you should stamp your feet to scare away snakes, but I was not sure if elephants would appreciate that. After all, I was in their space, and most likely they'd be really annoyed if I made more noise than necessary.

Forest ranger friends had told me that if they needed to put up a sign in the jungles they had to cover it with sharply pointed nails or else the wild elephants, seeing something man-made, would immediately pull it up with their trunks and throw it the way discus champions do at the Olympics. With my weight, they wouldn't be able to throw me very far, but I could make a very squishy lump underfoot.

I thought discretion would be the better part, not of valor in this case, but of not annoying elephants so I tiptoed the rest of the way, my ears fine-tuned to hear any snapping twigs. I walked on for perhaps only a few more yards that seemed like miles. Suddenly, I heard a voice intoning some blessings ... a monk! A monk up ahead!

I almost skipped the rest of the way and turning a sharp corner came upon a group of women talking to an elderly monk inside a small wooden pavilion. Behind the monk I could see a wide, deep hole, its sides lined with old, green bricks and filled with clear water. I was finally at the well.

The women turned and stared in surprise at my hurried entrance. They had just finished making an offering to the monk and were preparing to leave. Then one of them suggested to the others that they should wait for me so that I would not be alone on my way back ... I could have kissed them.

I trotted up to the monk and, as politely as I could in my hurry, asked him about the moving grass. Apparently he could not hear me, since he didn't reply but instead gave me his blessing. Although I appreciated being told that I would be healthy and wealthy, right now all I wanted was to see grass that walked, or perhaps even danced. I made little hops in my impatience while he continued to bless me.

Finally one of the kindhearted ladies came to help, and with our combined shouting he was able to hear us at last. Nope, he had never heard of moving grass. Didn't I want sacred water? Why hadn't I brought a bottle?

I was devastated. Probably the old man had already left for the day and I would never see him because I was going home the next morning. Waving away any offers of magic water, I wrapped a thousand kyat in a tissue and gave it to the monk. I did not wait for his blessing, for I had already received it three times and I did not want to delay the ladies. The sun would soon be setting.

To my dismay, long before the place of the terrifying poo, they turned left to go to a standing Buddha image, which stood on the very top of a really, really steep hill. I declined their invitation to go with them, thanked them, and walked off.

"You're so brave!" one of them called after me. Huh. Little did they know my knees were about to give way, but I made it safely back to the top of the winding lane leading down to the beach.

There was a descending shortcut that was very steep. I stood trying to decide if I should risk taking it when a woman of about seventy came up, very thin but spry with a large bundle balanced on her head, another on her hips, and a bag slung from her shoulder. She turned toward the shortcut and, seeing me dithering there in a cowardly fashion, said:

"I'll help you. Just follow me."

I was three times her weight, so it was either very brave or fool-hardy of her to take the chance of being toppled head over heels by me if I should fall. I stepped down the rugged incline, placing my feet carefully with each step, while my new friend walked slowly ahead of me. Finally we reached the bottom.

She was bringing back "stuff" from her daughter's shop, she told me, and then grumbled, "All these errands. I haven't even had lunch yet."

It was nearly sunset!

I went up to her and, putting one arm around her shoulders, gave her a squeeze.

"Listen," I told her, "You got me down that hill, and if you hadn't been there I might have fallen. I think of you as family, okay? So I'm treating you to lunch."

With that I slipped two thousand kyat into her bag and walked away.

I breathed easier now that I was on level ground and wandered over to the water's edge. I took off my slippers and small waves tickled my feet. The sea breeze was cool, ruffling the edge of my longyi while drying my brow. The sky was turning a grey-pink, with swathes of lavender.

I could see the sun, by now a deep orange, descending behind the Mawtin Zun Pagoda. The spire and hill stood out in a stark silhouette. I could almost imagine, as I often do when seeing the sun about to set, that it was calling for me to come along.

Hurry, hurry! It was saying. There were other lands beyond, and I might see the late afternoon, morning, or even the sunrise if I flew fast enough. But wingless, and with my soul still in captivity inside my body, I remained earthbound.

I walked into the waves, my compass in my hand, looking straight ahead toward the south ... to the Indian Ocean, vast, so vast, so empty; so desolate to think of being alone out there. I turned to face southwest, and there was the dragon's spur. Beyond his lair were India, Africa, and South America, places I have yet to see, people I have yet to meet, if I ever do.

It was suddenly darker; the sun had disappeared and the pale lavender that had washed both sea and sky had slowly deepened to dark velvet blue. I had reached the end of my river. I turned, still clutching my compass, and began to make my way back home.

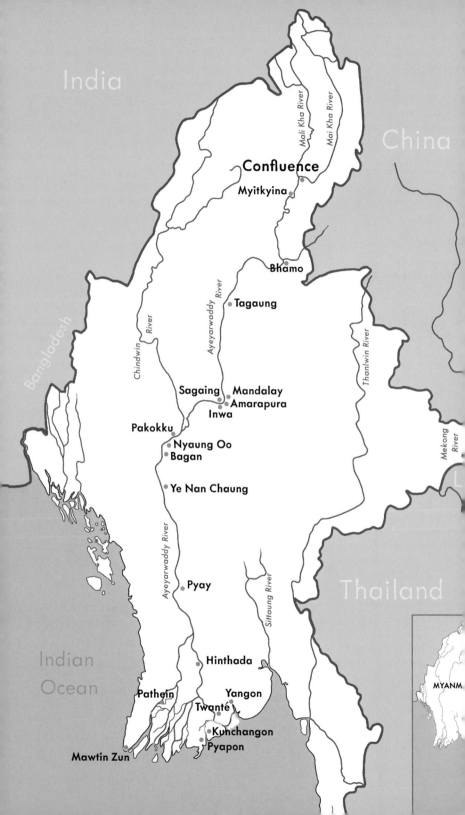

Ma Thanegi has written about a dozen books on Things Myanmar.

She is curious about everything, especially the food, arts, and culture of her country. Her motto regarding information is "it might come in useful one day." With that in mind she tries to find out as much as she can about places and people she comes across during the various periods of her life which, so far, include fanatic painter, dignified wife of a Myanmar diplomat, party-animal divorcée, and political prisoner, at which point she had the chance to make friends with hookers, pickpockets, and murderesses.

In her next life she is determined to come back as a cat because humans have to go to school and learn math and she's not going through that crap again.

She lives in Yangon.

Marmalade and Ma Thanegi

Appreciation

There are many people I must thank with heartfelt gratitude: again, and as always, U Sonny Nyein of Swiftwinds Services, who started me on my writing career; Phyu Mon and Chan Aye for their hospitality and art in Mandalay; Ko Maung Maung Saw and Ma Maw of Bagan House Lacquerware Shop for making sure I got on the cargo boat; Ma Hlaing and Kyaw for warm care and delta trips; Ma Ma, Bob, Gabriele, Sylvia, Karin, Marie, Anton, Ross, Wendy, and Maureen for their generosity toward the cyclone victims; Dr. Aung Myat Kyaw, Andrea Massari, and all on the RV Pandaw; Khin of Road to Mandalay for frequent invites; Janet Brown, angel, editor, and friend, for her support and enthusiasm; Albert Wen, my Archangel of Goodness; Don Gilliland of Dasa Book Café who got Janet, Albert, and me together; kind people who offered steadying hands on wobbly gangplanks and up steep banks; and not least, the many strangers with ordinary lives and decent values whose proud spirits, generosity, and warm hearts made sure I would never lose faith in the spiritual wealth of my country.

An Explanation of Male and Female Courtesy Titles as Used in Myanmar

Ko is a male prefix, used informally or for men of a lower status than the speaker.
Ma is used in same manner as Ko but for women.

U is a formal male prefix, used for older men or those of a higher status than the speaker or for strangers who are not young, to show respect.
Daw is used in same manner as U but for women.

Literally, **Ko** means "elder brother" and **U** means "uncle."
Literally, **Ma** means "elder sister" and **Daw** means "aunt."

Between close friends of the same age prefixes are not necessary.

THINGSASIAN PRESS

Experience Asia Through the Eyes of Travelers

"To know the road ahead, ask those coming back."
(CHINESE PROVERB)

East meets West at ThingsAsian Press, where the secrets of
Asia are revealed by the travelers who know them best. Writers
who have lived and worked in Asia. Writers with stories to tell
about basking on the beaches of Thailand, teaching English
conversation in the exclusive salons of Tokyo, trekking in
Bhutan, haggling with antique vendors in the back alleys of
Shanghai, eating spicy noodles on the streets of Jakarta,
photographing the children of Nepal, cycling the length of
Vietnam's Highway One, traveling through Laos on the mighty
Mekong, and falling in love on the island of Kyushu.

Inspired by the many expert, adventurous and independent
contributors who helped us build **ThingsAsian.com**, our
publications are intended for both active travelers and those
who journey vicariously, on the wings of words.

ThingsAsian Press specializes in travel stories, photo journals,
cultural anthologies, destination guides and children's books.
We are dedicated to assisting readers in exploring the cultures
of Asia through the eyes of experienced travelers.

www.thingsasianpress.com

To Myanmar With Love
A Travel Guide for the Connoisseur
Edited & with contributions by
Morgan Edwardson
Photographs by Steve Goodman

Tone Deaf in Bangkok
(and other places)
By Janet Brown
Photography by Nana Chen

To North India With Love
A Travel Guide for the Connoisseur
Edited & with contributions by Nabanita Dutt
Photographs by Nana Chen

Exploring Hong Kong
*A Visitor's Guide to Hong Kong Island, Kowloon,
and the New Territories*
By Steven K. Bailey
Photographs by Jill C. Witt

Communion
A Culinary Journey Through Vietnam
By Kim Fay
Photographs by Julie Fay Ashborn

Lost & Found Hong Kong
Edited by Janet McKelpin
Photographs by Hank Leung, Albert Wen, Blair Dunton,
Elizabeth Briel, and Li Sui Pong

Vignettes of Taiwan
*Short Stories, Essays & Random Meditations
About Taiwan*
By Joshua Samuel Brown

The Sushi Book
Everything About Sushi
By Celeste Heiter
Photography by Marc Shultz